Top 6 American Patriotic Books for 2018

Full of great information to help us all be better Americans

We did our part in bringing all of these patriotic solutions to you in their full versions and now again in this Whitman's Sampler, CliffsNotes-like version. In each chapter of this sampler, you'll find an introduction, followed by a Preface and a few chapter pieces. To differentiate chapters of the patriotic book from the synopsis books, we use a Ch designator rather than the word Chapter, followed by the Chapter number. That's all we need right here for an intro. A more detailed intro is provided in Chapter 1. Here are the titles of the Top 6 American Patriotic Books for 2018. Enjoy!

- *The Bill of Rights by Founder James Madison* The story of the Bill of Rights and a detailed look at each one.
- *The Founding of America* The essential American story from pre-colonial to post-revolutionary times
- *Winning Back America* The Days of Americans as Political Chumps Are Over!
- *The Constitution Companion* A guide to reading and comprehending the constitution of the USA
- The Constitution by Hamilton, Jefferson, & Madison From the pen of the founders – the Constitution
- *It's Time for the John Doe Party!* Can we still count on Republicans for the heavy lifting?

BRIAN W. KELLY

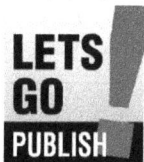

LETS GO PUBLISH

Copyright 2018   Brian W. Kelly
Title: *Top 6 American Patriotic Books for 2018*
Editor   / Publisher   Brian P. Kelly
Author   Brian W. Kelly

Disclaimer: Though judicious care was taken throughout the writing and the publication of this work that the information contained herein is accurate, there is no expressed or implied warranty that all information in this book is 100% correct. Therefore, neither LETS GO PUBLISH, nor the author accepts liability for any use of this work.

Trademarks: A number of products and names referenced in this book are trade names and trademarks of their respective companies.

Referenced Material: *The information in this book has been obtained through personal and third-party observations, interviews, and copious research. Where unique information has been provided or extracted from other sources, those sources are acknowledged within the text of the book itself or at the end of the chapter in the Sources Section. Thus, there are no formal footnotes nor is there a bibliography section. Any picture that does not have a source was taken from various sites on the Internet with no credit attached. If resource owners would like credit in the next printing, please email publisher.*

Published by: LETS GO PUBLISH!
Publisher: Brian P. Kelly
Editor: Brian P. Kelly
P.O Box 621 Wilkes-Barre, PA   www.letsgopublish.com

Library of Congress Copyright Information Pending
Book Cover Design by Brian W. Kelly

ISBN Information: The International Standard Book Number (ISBN) is a unique machine-readable identification number, which marks any book unmistakably. The ISBN is the clear standard in the book industry. 159 countries and territories are officially ISBN members. The Official ISBN For this book is also on the outside cover: **978-1-947402-30-0**

The price for this work is: **$8.95 USD**

10   9   8   7   6   5   4   3   2   1

Release Date: January 2018

LETS
GO
PUBLISH !

Dedication

I dedicate this book to my wonderful wife Patricia; our three wonderful children Brian, Mike and Katie; and our friendly friends—Ben our very happy dog, who recently became an Angel, and Buddy, our always cheerful cat.

Thank You All!

Acknowledgments

I appreciate all the help that I have received in putting this book together as well as all of my other 146 other published books.

My printed acknowledgments had become so large that book readers "complained" about going through too many pages to get to page one of the text.

And, so to permit me more flexibility, I put my acknowledgment list online, and it continues to grow. Believe it or not, it once cost about a dollar more to print each book.

Thank you and God bless you all for your help.

Please check out www.letsgopublish.com to read the latest version of my heartfelt acknowledgments updated for this book. FYI, Wily Ky Eyely loves this book and recommends it to all. Click the bottom of the Main menu!

Thank you all!

Preface:

Brian W. Kelly enjoyed putting this book together. Being the author of each of the six books, which outline the major patriotic books written for Americans today, made it easy for Brian to pick and choose the synopses that would be in this Whitman's Sampler / CliffsNotes patriotic book version.

Brian's objective was to put in one condensed book a compendium of his top patriotic books written in 2017 for 2018. With low ratings for the Hollywood self-aggrandizement shows and with historically low ratings for NFL games once the NFL went south on America, Brian believes that he has produced an antidote book for Americans suffering from a lack of patriotism around them.

By putting his six pro-American books in one quickly readable package, he feels that he has done his part to bring back many Americans who love the country deeply by basically saying that it is OK to love America again.

These CliffsNotes-like mini versions of his most popular patriotic books will put a big smile on the faces of all patriots and set the stage for those needing all the detail to run out to amazon.com/author/brianwkelly to find the full book versions of any and all and even more of these well-done patriotic books by Brian W. Kelly. Heck, you might even find a great Brian Kelly football book or two out there when you are checking things out on Amazon.

Kelly is very happy that he was able to put a nice package together for Americans who love America.

Why did Brian W. Kelly write this book?

Brian W. Kelly saw the problems with millennials and the problem with the negative influences of coffee breath college professors on America while he served as a college professor himself. He cares about America, millennials, and anybody being allowed to poach in America. He has great empathy for American taxpayers who are carrying the big burden of supporting those who choose not to chip-in.

Brian loves America and like President Trump, he wants America to be great because great Americans, who are permitted to live without government constraints, are the vehicle which will make America and all Americans great again.

You will love this book because it helps strengthen the will of Americans to fight against corrupt politicians and others trying to put US down. Kelly believes that knowledge of America is key to fighting off perpetrators that would be happy to bury US. In this package, those with little time, get to gain a great perspective in a short, Whitman's Sampler / CliffsNotes version of a detailed patriotic book.

Thank you for being so nice as to purchase this book and for helping keep America as the only place in the living world where freedom matters more than anything else.

I wish you the best.

Brian P. Kelly, Publisher
Wilkes-Barre, Pennsylvania

Table of Contents:

About the Author

Brian W. Kelly retired as an Assistant Professor in the Business Information Technology (BIT) program at Marywood University, where he also served as the IBM i and Midrange Systems Technical Advisor to the IT Faculty. Kelly designed, developed, and taught many college and professional courses. He continues as a contributing technical editor to a number of IT industry magazines, including "The Four Hundred" and "Four Hundred Guru," published by IT Jungle.

Kelly is a former IBM Senior Systems Engineer and IBM Mid Atlantic Area Specialist. His specialty was designing applications for customers as well as implementing advanced IBM operating systems and software facilities on their machines.

He has an active information technology consultancy. He is the author of 146 books and numerous technical articles. Kelly has been a frequent speaker at COMMON, IBM conferences, and other technical conferences.

Brian was a candidate for US Congress from Pennsylvania in 2010 and he brings a lot of experience to his writing endeavors.

Brian Kelly knows that by understanding the notions of the founders regarding patriotism and freedom, all Americans will be safer.

Chapter 1 Patriotic Books Are Inspiring

Football, Patriotism, and Domestic Policy

Brian W. Kelly, your author spent the first part of 2017 writing 12 sports books, beginning with three books about Alabama Football; three about Clemson Football; three about Florida Gators Football, and then he wrapped up the summer with three books about Army Football. He especially likes to write about the great moments, great coaches and great players in the football programs of fine American universities.

At the end of the summer, when the football season began, Kelly put the sports books to rest until the beginning of 2018. This year, his plan is to write about Syracuse, Navy, and Georgia.

After Brian took a respite from sports books, in the fall, he began to write new books and or update patriotic books and then he put together ten major domestic policy books.

For him, 2017 was a most productive writing year and I believe he has solved many of the domestic policy issues plaguing our nation for a number of years. If you find his newest book, *Top Ten American Political Books for 2010* on Amazon and Kindle, I hope you think he has accomplished that mission.

At the end of 2017, Kelly began to write the above referenced political book, the purpose of which is to present the ten solutions brought forth in his post-football books in a CliffsNotes style. Each of the ten domestic policy books in summary is a chapter in his Top Ten book.

Kelly also wrote the six patriotic books highlighted within during the same time period. Like the domestic policies book, this book contains synopses of six books that are simply good reading for 2018. They are perfect short-reads for anybody who wants to freshen up on their knowledge of America.

And, so this book is intended to be a presentation vehicle for six patriotic books that we hope you enjoy as much as Brian enjoyed writing them. 2017 was a great writing year for Kelly as a writer.

As he walked through his completed domestic policy books from the fourth quarter of 2017, he set the stage to have the armaments ready so that the solutions could be readily presented. Thus, Congress and the President would be able to slam through the legislation necessary to implement the major notions as described.

Your author has been overwhelmed by the support he received from family and friends and from his local Congressman. Brian Kelly knows that we can solve all of the problems outlined in his books if we keep our will and our wits about these very important issues.

After the sports books, before he went right back to work on better articulating the solutions to domestic issues that the best of the best in America had wrestled with for years, Kelly looked at a number of other books that he had written that were patriotic in nature without problem solving as a main theme. He created the following patriotic books. The book you are now reading is a compendium of these six books in one package:

- *The Bill of Rights by Founder James Madison* The story of the Bill of Rights and a detailed look at each one.
- *The Founding of America* The essential American story from pre-colonial to post-revolutionary times
- *Winning Back America* The Days of Americans as Political Chumps Are Over!

- *The Constitution Companion* A guide to reading and comprehending the Constitution of the USA
- The Constitution by Hamilton, Jefferson, & Madison From the Pen of the Founders – The Constitution
- *It's Time for the John Doe Party!* A look at the two-party system with a question-- Can we count on Republicans for the heavy lifting?

The next six chapters show the books referenced above, one chapter at a time. Thank you. Here goes:

Chapter 2 The Bill of Rights by Founder James Madison

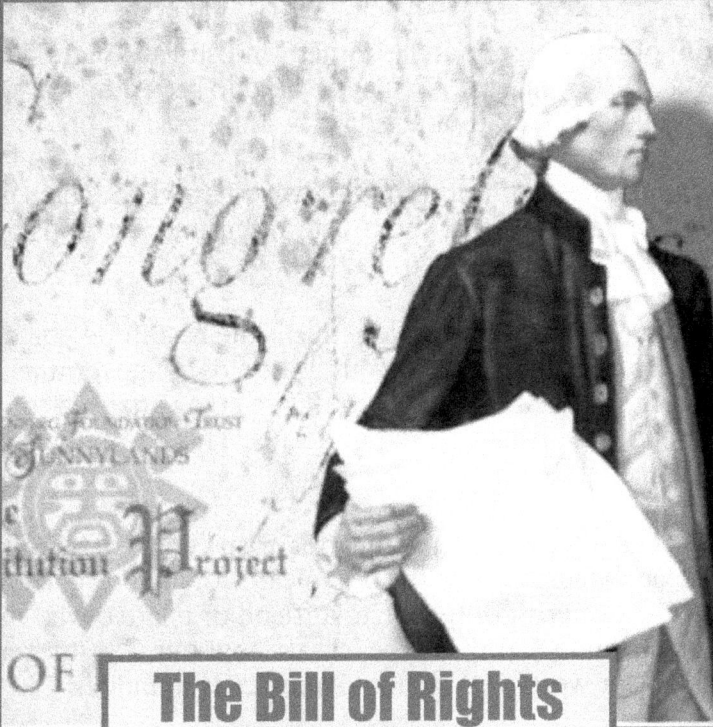

**The Bill of Rights
By Founder
James Madison**

Refresh your knowledge
of the specific rights
granted to all Americans

Brian W. Kelly

Refresh your knowledge of the specific rights granted to all Americans.

Book purpose

Read the Bill of Rights by Founder James Madison so you understand your rights & your freedoms…so that no nerd in government can take them from you! This book is unabridged & annotated.

Americans who hate corruption should love what the founders gave us in The Bill of Rights. Learn about your rights and freedoms by reading The Bill of Rights.

After understanding the Constitution, this is the best thing you can do to understand your role in assuring our great form of government. Our nation, our freedom and our liberties are being attacked today by corrupt left-leaning anti-American politicians. This book is one of the tools needed to stop them.

It does not get any better than reading this crisp copy of The Bill of Rights by James Madison. It is the best means for anybody who is reengaging with America or to give to a friend or relative who needs a nudge to understand what would be lost without our Constitution and Bill of Rights… or worst yet, without America as founded.

Know your rights!

Even if you learned civics years ago, knowledge of which, by the way, is hard to find today, more than likely you are unsure of what America offers in the way of rights, and powers, and the duties for Americans to achieve them. This book has been written as a first step to help you be better prepared to react to the over-reach of corrupt politicians at the highest levels of government. Know your rights or lose your rights!

Without the knowledge that you can gain easily in this book, for example, you might think that your representatives in Congress hold all the cards, and that mum is the word. You may think that you can speak freely only in the free speech zones of American universities. If you feel pressure to behave in a politically-correct fashion, this book is your first antidote to coming out of the funk and the group-think, and thinking again for yourself.

Just because powerful elite officials, who are part of the corrupt establishment in both political Parties choose to ignore our rights and freedoms does not mean we must endure tyranny. The first step of course is to understand the most basic written precepts in the Constitution and the fully described Bill of Ten written by Patriot President James Madison well before he ascended to the presidency of the USA. Madison would tell you that today ladies & gentlemen, reading this book is a must.

Table of Contents

Preface

We need to know our rights if for no other reason than to deny our politicians the opportunity to take them from us. Sometimes our current corrupt officials forget, that there are more of us than them so please do not get hoodwinked believing any of their self-serving spiel. They have no power but for what the people grant them. And we can un-elect on a regular basis and they are finished.

Once we the people are back in the game of life, knowing our rights, nobody will be able to take them away.

In a world where out of nowhere, one-day white people began to be labeled as supremacists and a curse for having experienced a white birth now causes a disease called white privilege. One wonders what went wrong. Having been brought up accidentally white, to believe that all men are created equal, I have no room for white supremacists, nor black supremacists, but it seems too many do. And a lot of that can be blamed on a wicked press and our poor leadership.

There are actually those who ask, "Why should Americans have lives that are nice when the rest of the world is suffering?" Ask yourself, what part of your personal America are you willing to give up for nameless, faceless, people who could care a hoot about whether you live or die. From the founding, Americans fought for everything we may have today. Our fortune came from hard work, guts, and not happenchance. The Bill of Rights are a monument to the thinking of the founders that all Americans, Asian, Black, or White can live in a world in which freedom for all is our calling card.

That's what it is all about today, folks. I hope that is why you are reading this book, written to counteract the influences of corrupt dirty politicians. This book uses the rights written by one of our greatest founders, James Madison, as a major tool against the rampant political corruption of today.

Why are the US press and the bulk of government workers so anti-American? Can you figure that one out? Black, Yellow, Red, or White, maybe they should take up residence someplace else and torment another group of people.

Early Americans fought for our rights and later Americans fought to preserve them. Communists were never interested in protecting our rights in the beginning, the middle, and surely not now when many non-thinking Americans are prepared to hand our country over to the corrupt people in our government who represent them.

So, what rhetoric would you expect from those that espouse an ideology that says government should take from you so that Joe Dokes down the street should never have to worry about working? Joe Dokes will never have any rights other than the short term right to not work for his meager welfare payments.

Since neither Communism nor communism has ever worked in any country, you and I know that life won't always be sweet for Joe Dokes and Mary Dokes. However, neither Joe nor Mary know it and they would not believe you if you read the history of the world to them 100 or more times.

American rights are not a gift. They were not donated to Americans by anybody. Many Americans fought, and many died for independence from the tyranny of England as well as in World Wars and other wars. America was always on the side of right and our great country still is on the side of right.

Once our own independence, freedoms, and liberties were gained from the bloodshed, the objective always was to keep the rest of the world safe and permit the whole world to live as well as it could in safety. America is a good country. America and Americans have helped our neighbors across the world from the moment our country was founded.

The graves of our sons and fathers and grandfathers with tombstones stretched across the world are vivid proof of our kindness as a country and our desire to help all the people of the world to become or to remain free. Don't let the *Blame America First* crowd talk down America while you are in the room. America and Americans deserve better.

Americans should not have to apologize to anybody. We should have no guilt. Yet, our bought and paid for corrupt press and our current corrupt government would love to ram tyranny down our throats by telling us we are bad people. Please don't buy any of it. We are not bad people.

We are exceptional people. Nobody has ever done, in the existence of recorded history, as much as America and Americans have done for our fellow man in America and across the world.

If you choose to wait until a Democrat, a progressive, a Marxist, or a communist says something good about America, you will be waiting a lifetime. Think about that while you consider if big government is really good for the people. Think again, please. Big government is good for big shots, big money, big corporations, big unions, a big corrupt press, and other big thinkers who hate America.

It has been 240 plus years since the United States, our country, achieved its independence. Along with independence, we the people, through the grace of our founders, earned freedom and liberty. Nobody has a right to demean US for that and nobody can take it away.

Ironically, there are some in America who espouse the liberal progressive Marxist ideology despite its demands that they give up on America. They are fully ready to blame America first for everything.

They hate you and I and I bet you they do not even know why! They probably do not like anybody including themselves and their "best friends."

Ironically, here we are, 240 some years after the Constitution and we still cannot get these people to agree that freedom is a good thing. Yet without freedom, they could not operate their clandestine socialist works in our country. As far as many Americans are concerned, it is OK if they all left town and went on to their favorite suppressed country to practice their ideology. They hurt America every day.

Though all is not perfect in America, the principles of the Constitution and the Bill of Rights are so sound and so powerful that even a knave politician cannot bring us under. The big concern of course is that if we all or at least if most of us do not smarten up, things will get a lot worse. I suspect that this is why you have chosen to read this book.

Our ailments have been large and growing in the past eight years. Taxes are still too high; elected officials are out of touch; government is too big; spending is out of control; the new healthcare program is a train wreck; the federal government is incompetent; the people have no voice in government; too many people are too lazy to hold government accountable; too many officials are on the take, and worse than that, the list of ailments is growing, not shortening.

Your intention no doubt in learning about the structure of America and its most fundamental laws, especially the Bill of Rights in choosing to read this book is to help you understand why all this is happening. Thank you. That is why my dad wrote this book. This book is fundamental to understanding your basic rights. From the founding. I am betting that more sooner than later, you will better understand our great country and our great form of government—at least before the bad guys take it away.

This book is the best starter book for anybody wanting to know how things really are and at the same time to refresh their knowledge or learn about the government of the United States of America. Those wanting to be better prepared to react to the over-reach of today's corrupt politicians at the highest levels of government will find this book gives them many answers. Without the knowledge that you can gain easily in this book, for example, you might not understand your rights. Then what?

If you have been paying attention, you know that as a country, we are in trouble. We have a busted economy, high unemployment, no jobs, and our basic rights to freedoms such as speech, religion, the press, and our right-to-bear-arms are being impinged upon. The founders saw it as a civic duty for Americans to pay attention to our government so that we can avoid being chumps and being snookered by crooked politicians.

There are more issues than just those noted above, and we better fix them quickly while we still have a Constitution and a Bill of Rights and a fine new President, upon which to lean.

Black, Yellow, Red, or White, we are on the same side in this battle for the Constitution, the Bill of Rights, and for the survival of America. Together we can all help. We first must understand what is going on and we then must understand our rights as delivered in the Declaration of Independence, The Constitution, and the Bill of Rights. This book focuses on The Bill of Rights as written as a set of amendments to our Constitution.

My concern is that when we all wake up from our deep fog, there may be no Bill of Rights or Constitution left for our progeny. We will have blown it for sure if that is permitted to happen.

In this book, Brian W. Kelly unabashedly recommends that we stop trusting government since it is clearly not working for our best interests. The sooner we can understand the threat from the left, the sooner we can move on to solving the problem for our values, our country, and our freedom.

The smarter we are, the more chance we have for success. Understanding America's founding and the founding documents, especially the Constitution and The Bill of Rights, is a sure way to become an American forever. I know you love America as I do.

Your author continually monitors what is happening to our government and he has written extensively on the major problems our country faces. Brian W. Kelly is one of America's most outspoken and eloquent conservative spokesmen. He is the author of *The Founding of America, The Constitution by Hamilton, Jefferson, and Madison, Sol Bloom's Epoch Story of the Constitution, No Amnesty! No Way!, Saving America, Taxation Without Representation, Kill the EPA!, Jobs! Jobs! Jobs!, and The*

Federalist Papers by the Framers, as well as many other patriotic books. All books are available at amazon.com/author/brianwkelly.

Like many Americans, Brian W Kelly, my dad, is fed up with stifling socialist progressive Marxists in the top seats in Washington. They place the needs of everybody else in front of the needs of Americans. Like many Americans, Kelly is shocked at how brazen the prior administration was in ignoring our Constitution and our Bill of Rights! This had to be stopped. In November 2016, the threats ended. We are all pleased with the new president's actions so far and we ask his fellow Republicans in Congress to get on the stick and make sure you support our President, or you will be gone soon.

Brian W. Kelly has read the founding documents, the underlying intelligence reports, and he has researched and written about such topics for years. Brian has written one hundred twenty-six books and hundreds of patriotic articles. He is deeply concerned about how intolerable the results of poor government policy can be within our neighborhoods and our lives. His comprehensible and sane recommendations in this book are explained in detail within the covers of this soon-to-be classic edition.

You are going to love this book, designed by an American for Americans. Few books are must-read, but *The Bill of Rights by Founder James Madison* will quickly be at the top of America's most read list.

Sincerely,
Brian P. Kelly, Editor
I am Brian W. Kelly's son

Ch 1 Americans Are Mad as Hell about Dwindling Rights!

Is it your job to give up your rights to others?

Today Americans on the left and the right are being asked to give up their rights so that others, who are jealous of those rights, can be made happy. Today's government leaders in both parties lean left and love to call themselves progressives. Being a progressive today gives some American rights that the founders never dreamed anybody would need or want.

For example, a progressive has the right to lie up a storm and he or she has the right to expect the corrupt media to swear that their word is the Gospel. A progressive can always say they did not take the cookie from the jar, even if their finger prints are all over the jar, and Lieutenant Columbo is saying: "Oh, oh, one more thing, before I forget..."

The point is that liberal progressives seem to have more rights than reality can imagine—including the rights to lie, to cheat, and to steal with impunity, especially if the real victim is a conservative.

The media enjoys covering for any lefty that lies. The low information crowd (LIC) has lost the ability to discern a lie from the truth. Therefore, lies do not affect the likeability or the electability of a politician. By the way, LICs cannot even discern the meaning of the word discern. That's why our country is in trouble. LICs brag about their lack of knowledge on most subjects when interviewed on the late-night TV celebrity road trips. But their dumbness is not really funny.

We live in a world in which real scandals are mocked as fake scandals and late-night TV hosts are supposedly the only ones who can tell a real scandal from a "fake scandal."

Some of the scandals about which we have learned from government and media sources are in the fake variety according to official government sources.

For the longest time, a sure way to throw off the LICs so they would always lean left was to blame Bush for everything imaginable. Ironically, now with Trump as the President, even the Bushes are blaming the new President and they have given the left a pass.

I do not want to be disrespectful to the institution of the US Presidency. Yet, many of us recall that when cornered, former president Obama often said that he got his news from the newspapers, not the White House Daily Briefing. Charles Krauthammer, a paraplegic who still has one of the sharpest mind on the planet, found this a bit problematic. These are his words:

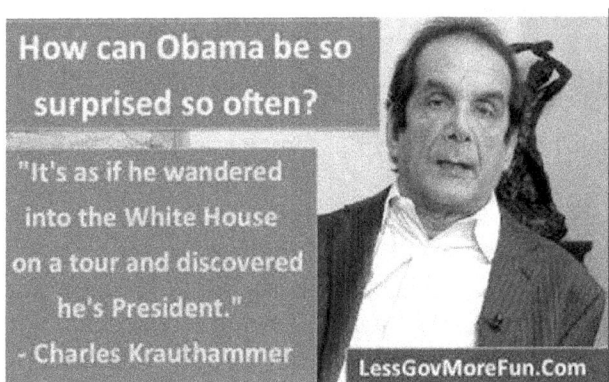

How can Obama be so surprised so often?

"It's as if he wandered into the White House on a tour and discovered he's President."

- Charles Krauthammer

LessGovMoreFun.Com

Every now and then, a Hollywood guy goes off the farm or as some say: "*off the reservation*," and insists on telling a new truth. This sometimes has the effect of making the old lies look like they too are true. It is a great trick and it can deliver a lot of laughs in Hollywood if delivered properly. Moreover, it can make the lefties seem smart at times.

Some elitists may say that only those Americans who are really stupid are unaware that the former president was really mad as hell that such things that he called "the fake scandals" could actually happen. They also suggest that this president would get even "madder" when he had to read the newspaper to find out about the fake scandals as his advisors seemed to want to concentrate on real scandals.

They "knew" he was working hard to make everything better— working really hard because he loves America deeply and his love of America is shared equally with, ahem, the First Lady. OK, maybe this paragraph was all fake.

Ch 2 The USA is a Constitutional Republic! A Representative Democracy

We have set the table well for this chapter. We now know that the United States is a suffering giant with caretakers who care more about their personal bank accounts than the people they represent.

None of us, even when we decide to act to save the nation, can do well in defending America without having facts at our disposal. Understanding the Constitution, which grants every right to the people except for a few select rights reserved for government such as building an army for defense and maintaining interstate highways, and regulating commerce between the states, and very few others, helps us know that we the people own America, not the government.

My sister Nancy is a very bright person, four grades ahead of me. She taught me the meaning of the word, redundant. We have a phenomenal Bill of Rights formed as the first ten changes (amendments) to our Constitution. These provide things like freedom of speech, religion, and a bunch of other rights including the right to bear arms.

The irony here is that the explicit Bill of Rights are redundant as all the rights in the Bill of Rights are provided implicitly in the Constitution itself. How is this? Simply by granting the people all rights other than those explicitly granted to the government, the default is that such rights as in the Bill of rights are for the people and thus are not dependent in any way on the government.

Nonetheless, extrinsically pronouncing these rights in the Bill of Rights made a lot of early Americans comfortable with the new government (Constitution replaced the Articles of Confederation) and today they make a lot of us comfortable that the government cannot pretend to have any of the rights deemed specifically for the people.

Amen!

Ch 3 Bill of Rights Says: Throws the Bums Out! Write opinion letters and call your representatives

The purpose of this book as noted from the beginning is to keep America as founded and to help US all be better Americans by understanding the Bill of Rights, an essential ingredient of the US Constitution. At the same time, as an adjunct to a greater understanding of our rights, we all need to learn a lot about America's founding. Most of us have heard of the Bill of Rights as an integral part of the US Constitution and when our rights are presented properly, we really like them. Who could say no to prosperity through liberty and freedom?

Many know the story of the Bill of Rights as it was actually an after-thought to the US Constitution—the defining document of our country. Doubtful patriots, who examined the Constitution for approval, wrote that all powers and rights not explicitly given to the government were held by the people. That means that the people own the government and not vice versa. So, let's say among other specific powers, the Constitution grants to the President, the Congress, and the Courts operating as the government the following powers / rights:

- ✓ To lay and collect import duties
- ✓ To pay the debts of the U.S. Government.
- ✓ To regulate commerce with foreign nations and Indian Tribes.
- ✓ To regulate commerce among the States.
- ✓ To regulate immigration
- ✓ To build roads and bridges
- ✓ To provide for the common defense (Army, Navy…), E
- ✓ Etc.

As you can see, these are things that we all would expect government to do as well as a number of other specific tasks all laid out in the Constitution. As you read the Constitution for free on the Internet or by a book by this author, you will notice that certain rights for government are not included; such as:

- ✓ Killing Citizens.
- ✓ Preventing the people from assembling in groups of more than two.
- ✓ Demanding that the people shop only at government stores.
- ✓ Requiring men to shave
- ✓ Preventing the people from eating on Tuesday.
- ✓ Etc.

Chapter 3 The Founding of America

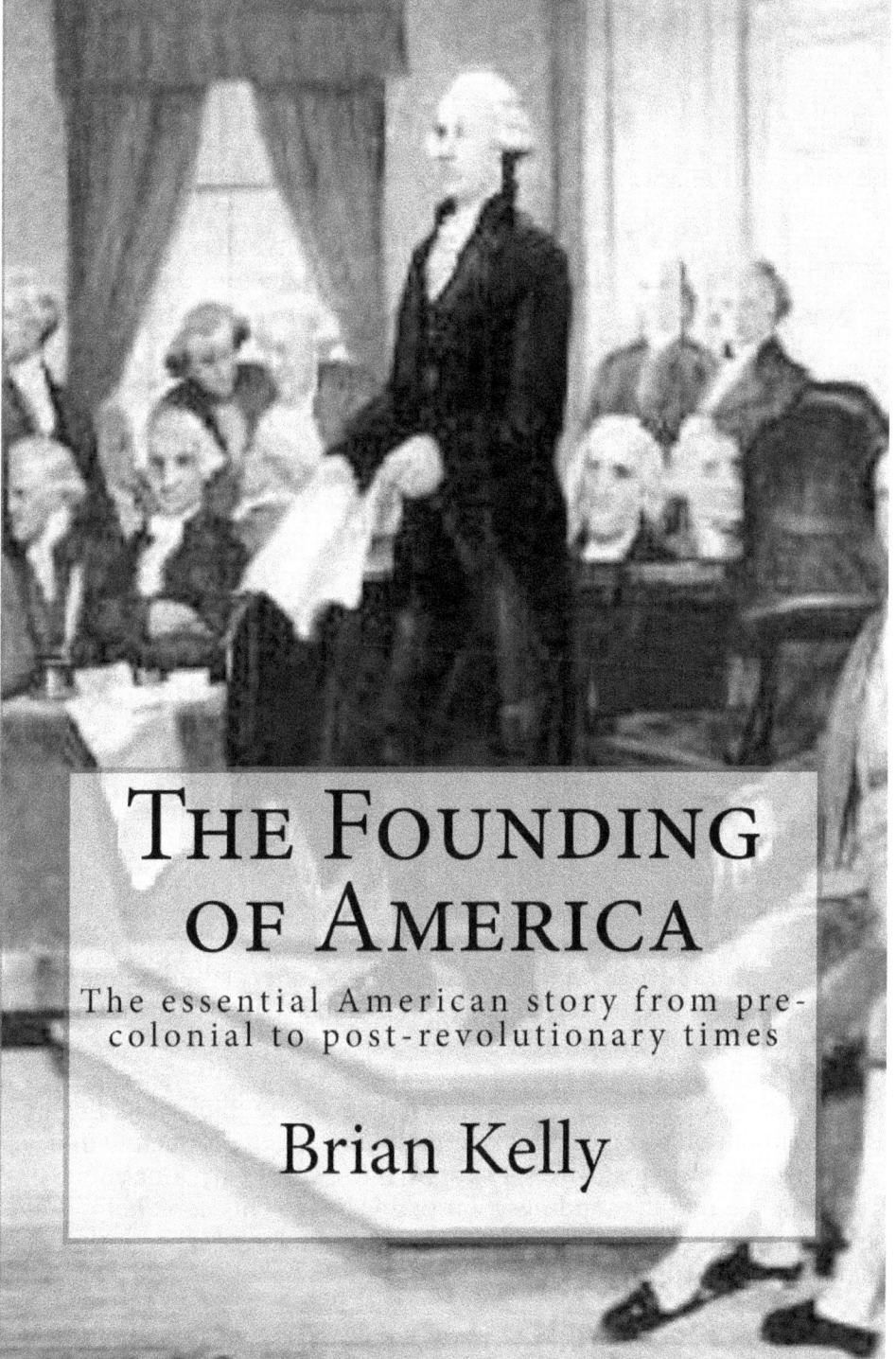

THE FOUNDING
OF AMERICA

The essential American story from pre-
colonial to post-revolutionary times

Brian Kelly

The essential American story from pre-colonial to post-revolutionary times

Book Purpose

Learn about America by reading The Founding of America. It is the best thing you can do to understand why everybody wants to live in America. This book is the best starter book for anybody wanting to refresh their knowledge or learn about America, its founding and how its basic principles of government assure freedom and liberty.

When Benjamin Franklin said: "We must indeed all hang together or most assuredly, we shall all hang separately," he gave away the essence of the seriousness of the task facing America's founders. For as trite as some seem to portray the founding today, it was a serious undertaking by serious men who had been pushed around enough by King George. There is no reason for anybody to be ashamed of America today or its founding. How lucky we Americans are with such great forefathers, and those who preceded them in the 1400's.

Our forefathers literally risked their necks so that we all could live free. America has been the greatest place on earth to live since its independence in 1776. The country was surveyed before 1492, and it was populated shortly after 1492 when it was known as the New World. In 1607, it became a colonial power and American settlements began to flourish.

Today, like other countries, we have our share of corruption and that is why we offer a primer on civics in this book after we take you back to the founding and we review our nation's most important documents. Americans have begun to fight corruption and are ready to win the battle. Learning about the founding is critical in this endeavor.

No matter how much sugar coating I might choose to provide, the fact is that our country and our government today is out of touch with its wonderful founding. It was not supposed to be this way. For you to fully understand the founding, I wrote this book. This book helps you see for yourself that our elected officials want to lord over us rather than be our servants as the founders intended.

This book begins a few hundred years before the founding and it shows today's Americans what early Americans endured for the sake of freedom and liberty.

This book teaches the discovery of our country through the American colonial period and through the formation of the American government. It is a quick way for you to learn about America and its many blessings and why its founding principles need not be replaced.

Just because corrupt and powerful people choose to ignore our rights and freedoms does not mean we must endure their tyranny. The first step of course is to understand the founding and the most basic written precepts describing America and our rights as Americans. Reading this book about America is a must for every US citizen.

Table of Contents

Preface

Here we are citizens in a truly exceptional country. Yet, even here in America all is not perfect. And so, our mission is to learn through civics lessons, light and heavy, that if we the people do not smarten up, things will get a lot worse and they may never get better again. This book is one of those trains that will take you where you want to go.

This is not a heavy book preaching about what you need to do to save America. I just finished a book like that called *Winning Back America*, which is one of the six books summarized in this book of synopses. Just because *The Founding of America* is mostly fact-based and not written as if Elmer Gantry himself were begging you to pay attention to your corrupt politicians, we do mention that once or twice in this book.

Why do we put you through that in a book that is mostly wonderful history about a wonderful brave people who risked everything to come to a wonderful new world? Well first of all, nothing is all wonderful. A big part of this book is about America being in bondage to Britain after taking a leap of faith to come here. Then, these wonderful and brave patriots were forced to risk their lives and their sacred honor to fight a revolution to gain their full freedom and our freedom from this oppressing nation. How's that for starters. Nothing in life worth having is easy!

No matter how anybody tries to make it sound, facts are facts. The fact is that our country and our government today is out of touch with its wonderful founding. It was not supposed to be this way. For you to fully understand the founding, I wrote this book. Now you can see for yourself that our officials have decided that instead of a country of the people, for the people, and by the people, politicians want to be the supreme rulers of America. They do not want to be our servants as the founders intended.

Here is what they have given us. Taxes are too high, elected officials are out of touch, government is too big, spending is out of control; the new healthcare program is a train wreck, the federal government is incompetent, the people have no voice in government, too many people are too lazy to hold government accountable, and finally too many of the nation's supposed best people are on the take. There's actually too much for the weak of heart not to become depressed.

The task you have just undertaken is to learn about America by reading this book. It is the best thing you can do to understand our great country and our great form of government, before the bad guys are empowered to take it away from us.

This book is the best starter book for anybody wanting to refresh their knowledge or learn about the pre-founding and the founding of America and the government of the United States of America. This book is a way that all citizens can use to be better prepared to react to the overreach of today's corrupt politicians.

Today more than ever with our former President and his coterie still trying to usurp the power of the new duly elected president, we citizens are in imminent danger. This book tells you what the deep state wants to take away from you. We advise you to keep saying. "NO," even if you like Oprah Winfrey.

We just went through a period in which the chief executive ignored the Constitution and administered the office of the presidency in a lawless fashion. We can never let this happen again. Americans need to know their rights and protections built into the basic framework of our government. This book is a great start in that direction.

The very worst thing we can do as Americans is give up these protections to a self-serving promise-everything group of elite liberal-progressive socialists. Our freedoms will be gone and will not come back on their own.

Just because one powerful group of people choose to ignore our rights and freedoms does not mean we must endure their tyranny. The first step of course is to understand America's discovery; its revolution, its founding, and its most basic written precepts. Reading this book is a must for every US citizen. You have more rights than you can possibly believe if your only sources of information are MSNBC, CNN, and the rest of the lying blatherskites.

If you have been paying attention to what is going on in America today, you know that we are in trouble. We have a busted economy, high unemployment, no jobs, and our basic rights to freedoms such as speech, religion, the press, and our right-to-bear-arms are being impinged upon. The founders saw it as a civic duty for Americans to *pay attention* to our government so that we can avoid being chumps and being snookered by crooked politicians. This book helps you relearn what civics is all about and why it is important to surviving in the new America.

You and I know that there are more issues than just those noted in this book, and we must fix them quickly while we still have an America. Isn't this a shame on US? I think that is why you bought this book. Thank you very much.

We are on the same side, and together we can all help. We first must understand what is going on and we then must understand our rights. Even before you and me, and everybody else are on board, you must start the first wave of solutions by opening your windows all the way and shouting as loud as you can: "I am mad as hell, and I am not going to take it anymore." Now, didn't that feel better?

Then, after you read this book, you must make sure that you talk to other citizens out there—those that you know—people like you and I and others, and let's help them know that it is time. It is time to get off the couch and act. Unless we all fully engage in America, an America explained in this book, when we wake up from our deep fog, there may be no America left for our progeny. We will have blown it for sure if we permit that to happen.

In this book, we unabashedly recommend that you stop trusting government, whether run by Republicans or Democrats, since it is clearly not working for our best interests. The sooner we can understand the active threat from the left and the passive threat from the right, the sooner we can move on to solving the problem for our values, our country, and our freedom.

It will be tough to wage this war against the corrupt politicians and the corrupt media if we are not even permitted to help on the battlefield when America is hanging by just a thread. The smarter we are, the more chances we have for success. Your knowledge is our best armament.

There is no question that a number of Americans—Democrat and Republican alike—have had enough. That is why Donald Trump is our new President. Trump represented everything that Americans viewed as a solution to the ills of government as practiced for many years— especially the eight years of a former anti-American president.

President Trump was different, and that difference gave him a big edge. He got the people tuned in and he won. Republicans are trying to undermine him along with Democrats. We need to un-elect them all.

President Trump pledged to "drain the swamp" of DC corruption, and he promised to renegotiate NAFTA, and build a wall to favor Americans over illegal aliens. The President also promised to repeal and replace Obamacare and rid the country of a burdensome tax system. and maybe that, too, will finally come to pass if Republicans help the President do his job.

Unfortunately, there are a group of people in his own political party and half of the Congress – the Democrats who have decided to not give the people the government we elected. And, so it is our duty to take what is not being given to President Trump. In this book, we explain how we got here from colonial times and what we can do about it from here on in.

Your author, Brian W. Kelly has been writing books to help Americans for years. He monitors what is happening to our government and he has written extensively in book form and in hundreds of articles about the major problems our country faces.

Kelly is one of America's most outspoken and eloquent conservative spokesmen. He is the author of *No Amnesty! No Way!*, *Saving America; Taxation Without Representation; Delete the EPA!; Jobs! Jobs! Jobs!; The Federalist Papers*, etc.—a total of 146 books. All books are available at amazon.com/author/brianwkelly in both paperback (Amazon) and eBook (Kindle) form.

Like many Americans, Brian was fed up with a stifling socialist progressive Marxist sitting in the top seat in Washington, DC. He is most thankful that God gave us Donald Trump to replace him. The progressives place the needs of everybody else in front of the needs of Americans. Like many Americans, Kelly is shocked and in some ways frightened at how brazen our former President had become in ignoring our Constitution.

Brian Kelly has read the founding documents, the underlying intelligence reports, and he has researched and written about such topics for years. As noted, Brian has written one hundred forty-six books and hundreds of articles. He is deeply concerned about how intolerable the results of poor government policy can be within our neighborhoods and our lives.

After walking us all through history and showing us the problems in government today, Kelly hopes that we will all seek out and find solutions. Some may be found in Kelly books; but our best hope is for that all Americans to not so readily accept the lies we are constantly being fed by the Democratic Party (Kelly, BTW is a Democrat) and the corrupt media.

More and more Americans are clamoring for jobs but for eight years, all that has been given by the government to the people has been lip service. Both parties permitted it. Donald Trump intends to end that and while doing that his plans will make America great again.

Trump wants Americans want to be able to keep or get their own health insurance and pick their own doctors, and he wants all Americans to be able to afford the insurance. If our past president had put his name to a plan like that, he might have won our support. Instead, the former president lied to the people and everything in his healthcare plan is worse than in 2009.

The Presidency is not the only area of national government that has been in trouble. Americans who know their rights voted out the party of the past president and must be ready to vote out scoundrels from the Congress and the Senate in Republican primary elections to protect America and Americans. A Congress that does not support the people's president must be voted out of office.

In his eight years, the prior president tried to take away our guns; ram a health scam on Americans that includes death panels for the elderly and infirm; grant illegals citizenship while handing them benefits paid by hard working Americans; and finally, he encouraged foreigners to take more American jobs. His party was punished by Americans in 2016 with the election of a president from the Republican Party, a newcomer, who is not ashamed of America, Donald J. Trump.

The Founding of America is a title to get your attention. In addition to reviewing the founding history, Brian W. Kelly has included a major civics lesson in this book to bring you up to date on the national scene. Additionally, he has referenced the founding documents and he shows how to bring them to your own device and read them.

You are going to love this book since it is designed by an American for Americans. Few books are a must-read but The Founding of America will quickly appear at the top of America's most read list.

Sincerely,

Brian P. Kelly, Editor

Ch 1 Introduction to Colonial History
Americans benefit from our democracy

Our Constitutional Representative Democracy, aka, our Republic comes from the hard-fought battles of the Revolutionary War plus the craft of our founders in writing our country's original laws. Everything America was and is, is because of the work of these great men who came before US.

Most Americans have a great feel for the notion of representative democracy and the sense that we elect representatives of the community to handle our affairs in the governing of the nation. We also have the privilege of a Constitution, which is intended to prevent tyranny by a government gone wild. We do not have a direct democracy in that we do not conduct the activities of government ourselves in Washington. Instead we use representatives.

It would be very difficult squeezing over 300 million people into a room in Washington D.C. Instead, we choose representatives among us to get the job done according to the Constitution.

What's next?

When you begin to think through how the country is in turmoil, your opinion of the purity of the act of representation may become tainted. That is OK. I am happy to generate some alarm and a sense of urgency among the readers for we simply may not have much time left to get it right.

Something surely went wrong with the intention of representation from the Founding Fathers to what representation means today. Something went way wrong sometime between the first documented ships in 1492 and the present day, but the evidence suggests that the problem began closer to the year 2000 than to the year 1400. That's not to say that all was hunky-dory in the 1400s and onward.

Let's now take a look how America started to set the initial stage for an explanation. Then, we will take a peek at the history of Colonial times and the times from our founding onward. Eventually we will look at current times but not in great detail. However, we will note that today, we most certainly suffer from the problems of corrupt representation.

Along the way from the beginning of our country, in this book, we will stop several times to examine important events that helped form our country and ultimately our government.

After we work through the original history of America, we move on to take a hard look at civics, a subject no longer highlighted in K-12 curricula. We will get a nice civics lesson on government choices that the founders made so we can better appreciate our republican form of democracy.

From here we will discuss some of the pitfalls that any government runs into, especially our Constitutional Republic after over 200 years in existence.

Chapter 4 Winning Back America

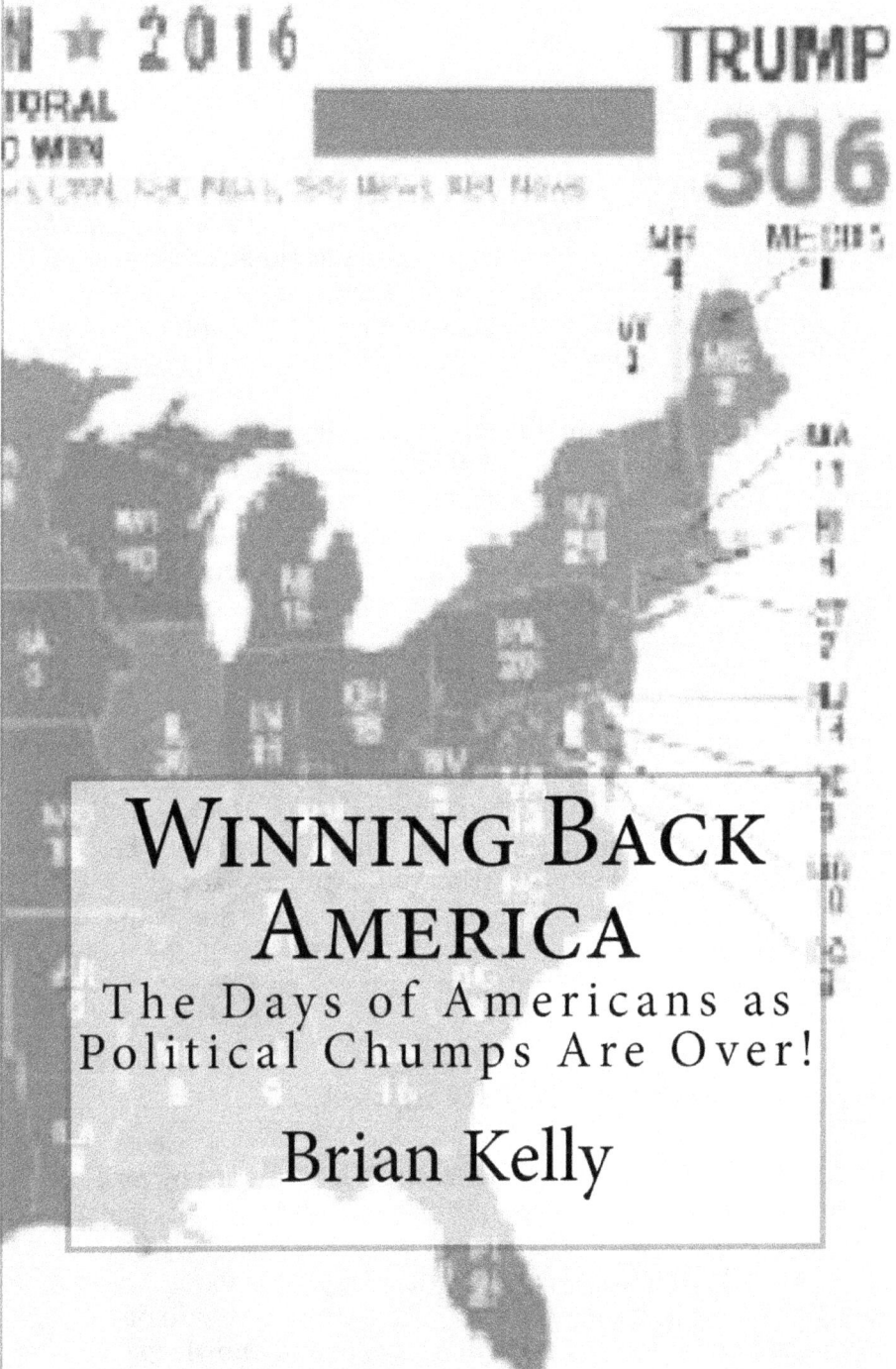

WINNING BACK AMERICA

The Days of Americans as Political Chumps Are Over!

Brian Kelly

The Days of Americans as Political Chumps Are Over!

Book Purpose

OK folks, raise your hand if you haven't been involved in politics in any way in the last 10 or 15 years? A typical reaction from an audience would be that half of the people would raise their hands. Did you raise your hand? These are exactly the type of Americans who have felt excluded from the process, who believed for so long that they had no power to change the course of this country. That is sad for sure.

I know that until I was in my fifties, I let running the country and electing the best people to others. I always voted but I did not pay attention to the news or read the paper all the time. Instead, like many of you, I was raising my family and working harder than I had to at my job to assure I would be able to pay the bills and put food on the table. I was tired when I got home and had little time for fun and had less time for anything political.

I was like many Americans, who even today are disaffected with politics and with politicians. Most people do not believe that politicians are responsive to them; they don't think government is on their side, and they are not particularly interested in the political process. This disaffection as much as an overall sense of helplessness must be responsible for a significant proportion of the public's lack of engagement. To get our country back from the elites, the swamp, the establishment, and too many corrupt politicians who call themselves our representatives, we need people to get involved again.

Know your country and its issues

I am very pleased that you chose to learn about America by reading *Winning Back America*. It is the best thing you can do to understand why everybody wants to live in America. This book is one of the best for anybody wanting to refresh their knowledge or learn about America, its founding and how its basic principles of government assure our freedom and liberty. It all starts with an aware and knowledgeable citizenry.

In introducing many of my books dealing with the founders, I like to quote Benjamin Franklin. You may recall these famous words: "We must indeed all hang together or most assuredly, we shall all hang separately." With these words, Franklin gave away the essence of the seriousness of the task facing America's founders. For as trite as some seem to portray the founding today, it was a serious undertaking by serious men who had been pushed around enough by King George. They simply were not going to take it anymore. There is no reason from anybody to be ashamed of America today or its founding.

Today, it is unfortunate that our country is led by too many corrupt and greedy politicians. They have taken control of many levels of governments in America. The good news is that the people are waking up slowly but surely. Donald Trump is a product of the wake-up call heard by Americans in the eight years of Obama's presidency. Americans have decided to no longer be chumps looking for alms at the politician's table. Nor are the people sitting idly by today as in the past hoping things will get better.

Americans are taking steps to gain back the freedoms lost as well as those that are being lost. Hop on the Train of Freedom folks to win back America from the forces of evil. Start right now and learn about America and what we can all do to keep her strong and vibrant.

This book is today's solution for would-be chumps to be better prepared to react to the overreach of praetorian politicians and elite establishmentarians, who hope to set the country back three hundred years.

Liberal socialist progressives in this grouping of American leaders are working to convince the people that government is more important than the people and that the founding was illegitimate. They have their own self-serving agenda to not only remove symbolic statues of our founders, but they also want to remove the Constitution and its guarantees of freedom. They would be happy to replace freedom with a hand-out based government that controls the people and not vice-versa.

There is not one political party that can be trusted to guard our freedom and liberty. Both elite Republicans and Democrats love the massive federal government and they hate state's rights and individual liberty. Their America would permit these rapscallions to bend hundreds of millions of people to their will with one imperial America-killing edict after another. Their objective is to turn our beautiful country into a third-world banana Republic, making all citizens dependents of the government for life. The lie is their favorite weapon. They must be stopped.

This book is a quick way for you to learn about how to win back our America and regain its many blessings. It shows why its founding principles need not be replaced.

Just because corrupt and powerful officials choose to ignore our rights and freedoms does not mean we must endure their tyranny. The first step of course is to understand the founding and the most basic written precepts describing America and our rights as Americans. Reading this book about America is a must for every US citizen.

Table of Contents

Preface

Here we are citizens in a truly exceptional country. Yet, even here in America all is not perfect. And so, if we the people do not smarten up, things will get a lot worse and they may never get better again.

Our country and our government are out of touch with its founding. It was not supposed to be this way. Taxes are too high, elected officials are out of touch, government is too big, spending is out of control; the new healthcare program is a train wreck, the federal government is incompetent, the people have no voice in government, too many people are too lazy to hold government accountable, and finally too many of the nation's supposed best people are on the take... There's lots more!

Learn about America by reading this book. It is the best thing you can do to understand our great country and our great form of government, before the bad guys are empowered to take it away from us.

This book is the best book for anybody wanting to refresh their knowledge or learn about the founding of America and the government of the United States of America. This book is a way that all citizens can use to be better prepared to react to the overreach of today's corrupt politicians.

Without the knowledge that you can gain so easily in this book, for example, you might unknowingly sign up for a socialist progressive government that takes away your rights, and makes you dependent on government employees for the rest of your natural life.

Today, we citizens are in imminent danger. We just went through a period in which our past president ignored the Constitution and administered the office of the presidency in a lawless fashion. We can never let this happen again. Americans need to know their rights and protections built into the basic framework of our government.

The very worst thing we can do as Americans is give up these protections to a self-serving promise-everything group of elite liberal-progressive socialists. Our freedoms will be gone and will not come back on their own.

If you have been paying attention to what is going on in America today, you know that we are in trouble. We have a busted economy, high unemployment, no jobs, and our basic rights to freedoms such as speech, religion, the press, and our right-to-bear-arms are being impinged upon. The founders saw it as a civic duty for Americans to *pay attention* to our government so that we can avoid being easily deceived and being suckered by crooked politicians.

You and I know that there are more issues than just those noted above, and we must fix them quickly while we still have an America. Isn't this a shame on US? I think that is why you bought this book. Thank you very much.

We are on the same side, and together we can all help, and we can win back our country. We first must understand what is going on and we then must understand our rights. Even before you and me and everybody else are on board, we must start the first wave of solutions. If you have read any other books of mine, you may have heard this admonition. Go ahead and open your windows all the way and shout as loud as you can: "I am mad as hell, and I am not going to take it anymore." Now, didn't that feel better?

After you read this book, you must make sure that you talk to other citizens out there—those that you know—people like you and I and others, and let's help them know that it is time. It is time to act. We can no longer wait for others to do our job. Unless we all fully engage in America, when we wake up from our deep sleep, who knows what will be left of our country. What then?

In this book, we tell you straight-out to stop trusting government, whether run by Republicans or Democrats. It has not been working, has it? Modern day politicos work for themselves and not for our best interests. The sooner we can understand the active threat from the Democratic Party attempting to win elections by enticing illegal foreign nationals to take over for regular Americans, the sooner we can move on to solving the problem for our values, our country, and our freedom.

There is no question that Americans in all political parties have had enough. My party, I am afraid, the Democrats, left me behind years ago. I believe when history begins to be written honestly that today's Democrat leaders will not look good. They are selling out Americans, so they can get the vote of illegal aliens. It is so simple to understand they stopped hiding it. Instead, they want the people to accept it as the right thing to do.

More and more Democrats said, "Enough," to a party that is willing to sacrifice Americans and their families for the foreign vote. That is why Donald Trump is our new president. Trump represented everything that Americans viewed as a solution to the ills of government as practiced for too many years—especially the eight years former anti-American president reigned over America. President Trump was different, and that difference gave him a big edge. The people saw the edge and elected him as the new leader of the free world.

Now, Americans must do the same for our representatives. This cannot go on. Democrats in the trenches must stop voting for Democrat politicians who want to ruin our country. Vote them out until the Democrats come up with a pro-American platform.

President Trump coined the term, "drain the swamp" of DC corruption, and he is being fought tooth and nail by Democrats who love the Swamp and never Trumpers who ought to become Democrats. The people must remain actively involved to keep our country from falling. I think we can win it all back if we tried.

It is our duty to take what is not being given to President Trump. In this book, we explain how we got here and what we can do about it from here on in.

Your author, Brian W. Kelly has been writing books to help Americans for years. He monitors what is happening to our government and he has written extensively in book form and in hundreds of articles about the major problems our country faces.

Kelly is one of America's most outspoken and eloquent conservative spokesmen. He is the author of *No Amnesty! No Way!*, *Saving America, Taxation Without Representation*, , *Kill the EPA!*, *Jobs! Jobs! Jobs!*, *The Federalist Papers*, etc.—a total of 146 books. All books are available at amazon.com/author/brianwkelly in both paperback (Amazon) and eBook (Kindle) form.

Brian Kelly has read the founding documents, the underlying intelligence reports, and he has researched and written about such topics for years. As noted, Brian has written one hundred twenty-five books and hundreds of articles. He is deeply concerned about how intolerable the results of poor government policy can be within our neighborhoods and our lives. After walking us through history and showing the problems in government today, Kelly's comprehensible and sane recommendations in this book are explained in detail within the covers of this soon-to-be classic edition.

The Presidency is not the only area of national government that has been in trouble. Americans who know their rights voted against the party of the former president and must now be ready to vote out the obstructionist scoundrels from the Congress and the Senate to protect America and Americans. A Congress that does not support the people's president must be voted out of office.

In his eight years, the former president tried to take away our guns; ram a health scam on Americans that includes death panels for the elderly and infirm; grant illegals citizenship while handing them benefits paid by hard working Americans, including free education; and finally, he encouraged foreigners to take more American jobs. His party was punished by Americans in 2016 with the election of a president from the Republican Party, a newcomer, Donald J. Trump.

Winning Back America is a title to get your attention. Brian W. Kelly knows that corrupt politicians want to make suckers and chumps out of all Americans, so they can advance their personal and group-think agendas. Kelly does not want Americans to trust the politicians from the Swamp. Like WC Fields, politicians are not about to give a sucker an even break or smarten up a chump. After the chapters in this book, you will no longer be content with being a sucker or a chump and you will work hard to win back America for the sake of freedom and liberty.

You are going to love this book since it is designed by an American for Americans. Few books are a must-read but Winning Back America will quickly appear at the top of America's most read list. If we do not win back our America somebody we do not like will own us?

Sincerely,

Brian P. Kelly, Editor

Ch 1 Mad as Hell About the US Government! I'm Mad as Hell!

The corrupt mainstream media has decided that its mission is to remove Donald Trump from Office and the quicker the better. Fake news and outright lies are their weapons of choice and they have a huge following of people who have been enjoying their work in trying to depose our president one way or another.

Though most Americans are not privileged, the media and the Democratic leadership and a large part of the Republican Establishment enjoy the fruits of political greed and the full benefits of the "Swamp." It's been like that for too many years to expect that anything, the purpose of which is the good of the country, would have any meaning to them.

The daily soap opera promulgated by this nasty press every day spews vile on the President and tries to convince weak-minded Americans that by jumping on their negative train they can gain back the great times from the last eight great Obama years. The press is actually worse than the far left in trying to persuade Americans to give up the Constitution and bring in a socialist regime.

Fixthisnation.com began their explanation for a new White House set of talking points intended to fight the fake news and it is the perfect way to begin this book because like everything including the fake *Russia collusion soap opera*, the press tells one fat lie after another. So far, Americans are not buying it and that is good.

"The White House issued talking points to allies in the Republican Party on Tuesday – talking points that are almost certainly going to be ignored by politicians who refuse to stand up to the media's ideological tyranny. As far as the mainstream right is concerned, President Trump is completely toxic at this point. Like rats from a sinking ship, Republicans are doing everything they can to distance themselves from the president, as if he REALLY IS the neo-Nazi, white supremacist that the liberal media insists that he is. It occurs to only a very, very select few that maybe – just maybe – it's just the media lying once again in an attempt to smear all of conservatism with the same racist brush."

"The president, said the issued talking points, were "entirely correct – both sides of the violence in Charlottesville acted inappropriately, and bear some responsibility." The memo went on to encourage Republicans to remind the press that Trump used "no ambiguity" in condemning the white supremacist groups that gathered for the rally at UVA and in the Town Square the next day. The White House asked allies to present President Trump as "a voice for unity and calm" and a leader "taking swift action to hold violent hate groups accountable." "

As Americans have begun to discern, the press is not only anti-Trump, they are anti-American, and they lie like the Devil to try to suck in weaker Americans into their doomsday party. Many Americans simply can't take it anymore.

I can't take it anymore

Do you remember back in November 1976 when Howard Beale, as played by Peter Finch, the long-time anchor in the movie "Network News," gets the bad news that eventually causes him to utter one of the most famous movie lines of all time? Beale gets fired and is given two weeks. The long-time anchor has a very poor reaction to this personal news and he cannot control himself during the next broadcast. He "goes off the deep end."

He promises to commit suicide on the air. The company immediately fires him—no second chances for a repeat performance. Beale is devastated and remorseful. He begs for the opportunity to say good-by to his fans with dignity, and he is given his last opportunity ever for air time so that he can say his good-by's respectfully and also apologize. Nobody expects it to happen, but Beale gets his chance, and it is billed as a last chance.

Despite his promises, once on the air, Beale is overwhelmed by his circumstance. He goes into another diatribe starting off with a rant claiming that "Life is bullshit." He is so passionate that his ratings spike as he persuades his viewers to shout out of their windows: "I'm as mad as hell, and I'm not going to take this anymore!" Like the shot at Lexington and Concord, this is the line heard round the world.

Well, my fellow Americans, I bet you saw this coming, and I am going to deliver it as passionately in words as I can: "I am mad as hell, and I am not going to take this anymore." I bet you are too.

Chapter 5 The Constitution Companion

The Constitution
Companion

The Constitution
Companion

Brian Kelly ❧

A Guide to Reading
& Comprehending
The **Constitution**

by

Brian W. Kelly

*A Guide to Reading and Comprehending The
Constitution of the United States of America*

A Guide to Reading and Comprehending the Constitution of the United States of America

A Companion Book: The Constitution by Hamilton, Jefferson, Madison, et al., written and edited by Brian W. Kelly is available on Amazon & Kindle

Study the Companion to learn the Constitution!

Learn the US Constitution by using this book as a companion to read and comprehend the Constitution of the United States. It is the best approach you can take to understand our great form of government.

This companion book serves as a guide to reading and understanding any unabridged edition of the Constitution as freely available on the Internet. Brian Kelly's book, titled, The Constitution by Hamilton. Jefferson, Madison, et al. is a very suitable edition, which is available in paperback or download form from Amazon or Kindle.

This Companion to the Constitution introduces the Constitution as an empirical guide for learning the basic law of the land. You will no longer need to rely on fake news or an outright lying media for your facts about what is right and wrong about government.

This book describes an easy means of understanding the nuances about the processes leading to the Constitution and it presents the Constitution in a highly understandable, highly readable fashion.

You won't be able to put this book down once you begin the learning process.

Table of Contents

Commentary / Preface

Welcome to the Lets Go Publish! edition of *The Constitution Companion*. This is Brian Kelly's 120th book! This original effort by the founders culminated in a document we all know as the Constitution of the United States of America. It was written, published, and ratified by the 13 states during the years 1787 and 1788 with some holdover states signing up later.

To help sell the Constitution to America, three primary authors, Hamilton, Madison, and Jay wrote 85 essays outlining how this new government would operate under the Constitution and why this Constitution defined the correct form of government for the United States.

The Constitution is a document that might be considered a small book or pamphlet but understanding the Constitution itself and understanding the words of the Constitutions in 2017 is not as easy as it might at first sound.

And, so, to better comprehend the purpose and meaning of the Constitution as the guiding set of laws for our nation, your author has written this companion book to the Constitution. You can find free downloadable copies of the Constitution on many Internet sites and there are books that fit in a suit pocket to regular sized books which tell the full story of this grand body of law.

Your author has a fine book available about the Constitution with the full text of four founding documents for your reading pleasure. You may acquire Brian W. Kelly's *The Constitution by Hamilton, Jefferson, Madison, et al,* at Amazon or Kindle. The Kelly book contains both an unabridged and much larger type version of the original Constitution document along with some helpful cues for understanding.

You may also access the Articles of Confederation, the precursor to the Constitution, as well as the text of the entire Declaration of independence and the Bill of Rights in addition to the text of the Constitution.

A tribute to the Constitution Society from their site follows. They would appreciate donations for their worthy cause:

Welcome to the
Constitution Society

This site aims to eventually provide almost everything one needs to accurately decide what is and is not constitutional in most situations, and what applicable constitutions require one to do. It is for constitutional decision support.

The Constitution Society is a private non-profit organization dedicated to research and public education on the principles of constitutional republican government. It publishes documentation, engages in litigation, and organizes local citizens groups to work for reform.

This organization was founded in response to the growing concern that noncompliance with the Constitution for the United States of America and most state constitutions is creating a crisis of legitimacy that threatens freedom and civil rights. Although the focus here is on government in the United States, coverage also includes the rest of the world, and private as well as public organizations. We maintain that the principles of constitutional republicanism are universal, and applicable to all nations, although not well understood or upheld by most. We also examine the related principles of federalism and nomocracy, the rule of law, of nomology, the science of law, and show how those principles are applicable to solving the fundamental problem of avoiding excessive or unbalanced concentrations of power.

Lets Go Publish! and your author thank the Constitution Society for its great work

Ch 1 Americans Are Not Happy with the US Government or the Press!
The format of this companion book.

After we demonstrate the need for the Constitution in the first several chapters of this book and we move on to discuss the purposes of the Constitution, and how this historically significant document came into being, we explain the text of the Constitution as we dissect it one block at a time. As a companion document to the Constitution itself, the major purpose is to explain the 18th century text of this short document so that it can be understood by those of us living in the 21st century.

How mad can we get with our government?

More and more Americans are upset today because our Constitution has been and continues to be under attack by left-wingers –liberals, socialists, and progressives in America.

The Constitution, the law of the land, which you are about to study, has been unlawfully bypassed by opportunists in the Federal Government.

Chapter 6 The Constitution by Hamilton, Jefferson, Madison, et al.

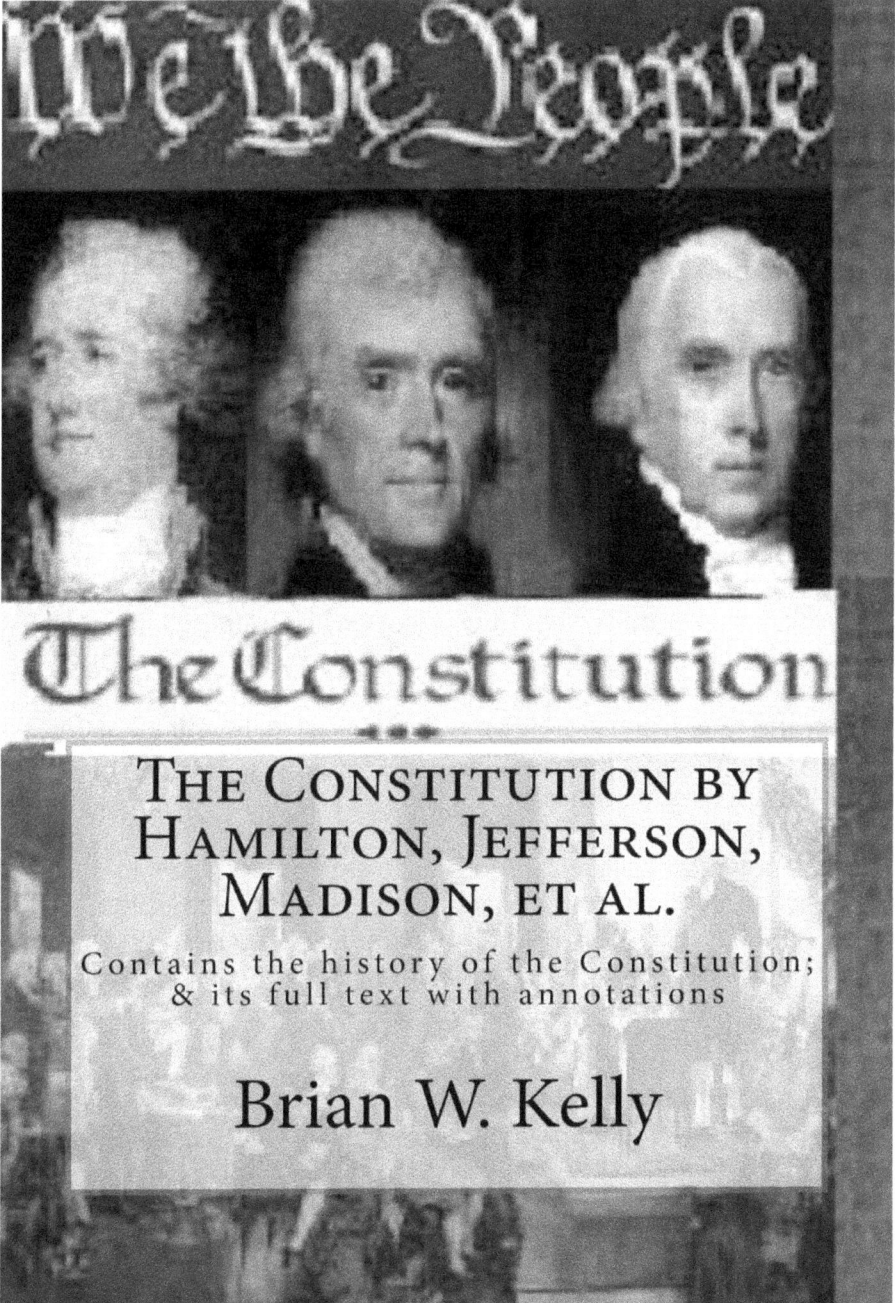

We the People

The Constitution

THE CONSTITUTION BY HAMILTON, JEFFERSON, MADISON, ET AL.

Contains the history of the Constitution; & its full text with annotations

Brian W. Kelly

Contains the history of the Constitution; as well as its full text with annotations. It highlights the story of the fight to assure its ratification as the governing document for the new United States.

This is your first book to read to help make the great words of the Constitution ring forever in your ears. We begin with the thinking of the major patriots who wrote this document—men such as Hamilton, Jefferson, and Madison, et al.

The book then moves on to the purpose of the Constitution; how it came about, and who the writers actually were. You will learn why the Constitution is the most famous written document of all time. The patriot founders so properly named it: "The Constitution of the United States of America." We are the lucky ones for sure as this is the definition of our democracy!

From this book about the Constitution, you will learn about your rights and freedoms by reading this great document. Understanding the Constitution is the best thing you can do to understand your role in assuring our great form of government well into the future.

This effort resulting from the combined work of Hamilton, Jefferson, Madison, and others is the best starter book for anybody wanting to refresh their knowledge or learn about the US government and its most basic structures and laws. This book is designed to help you be better prepared to react to the over-reach of corrupt politicians in our age, at the highest levels of government.

Just because powerful people for too long a time have chosen to ignore our rights and freedoms does not mean we must endure continual tyranny. The first step of course is to understand the most basic written precepts in the Constitution.

Therefore, reading this book is a must.

The Table of Contents

Preface

Indeed, we are citizens of a truly exceptional country. America is the exception to the rule, founded on principles of liberty and freedom and ruled by the people. The Founders knew that even the great Constitution they wrote might not be enough to keep knaves and scoundrels from subverting their work. Just check the news every day and you know how true this is. But, of course, be careful and watch out for the fake news.

And so, today, over 225 + years after the Constitution, all is not perfect in America, but the principles of the Constitution are so sound and so powerful that even a knave politician cannot bring us under. The big concern of course is that if we don't smarten up, things will get a lot worse. I suspect that is why you are reading this book, originally written by the Founders.

Our ailments are large and growing. Taxes are too high, elected officials are out of touch, government is too big, spending is out of control; the new which now is also the old healthcare program is a train wreck/ The Federal government is incompetent, the people have no voice in government. Too many people are too lazy to hold government accountable; too many are on the take, and worse than that, the list of ailments is growing, not shortening.

Your intention no doubt in learning about the structure of America as written by its founders—its most fundamental laws—in choosing to read this book is to help you understand why all this is happening.

That is why Brian wrote this book. I am betting that more sooner than later, you will better understand our great country and our great form of government—at least before the bad guys take it away.

This book is the best starter book for anybody wanting to refresh their knowledge or learn about the government of the United States of America and to be better prepared to react to the over-reach of today's corrupt politicians at the highest levels of government.

Without the knowledge that you can gain easily in this book, for example, you might unknowingly be convinced by socialist progressives in the government that you have no rights, and you have no freedoms, and any of your permissions come from the government itself. The Constitution itself says pay no heed to "fake news like this."

If you have been paying attention to what is going on in America today, you know we are in trouble. We have a busted economy, high unemployment, no jobs, and our basic rights to freedoms such as speech, religion, the press, and our right-to-bear-arms are being impinged upon. The Founders saw it as a civic duty for Americans to pay attention to our government so that we can avoid being chumps and being snookered by crooked politicians.

We are on the same side in this battle for the Constitution and for the survival of America. Together we can all help. We first must understand what is going on and we then must understand our rights as delivered in the Declaration of Independence, The Constitution, and the Bill of Rights.

My concern is that when we all wake up from our deep fog, there may be no Bill of Rights or Constitution left for our progeny. We will have blown it for sure if that is permitted to happen.

In this book, Brian Kelly unabashedly recommends that we stop trusting government since it is clearly not working for our best interests.

The sooner we can understand the threat from the Left, and how our President is on America's side, the sooner we can move on to solving the problem for our values, our country, and our freedom.

The smarter we are, the more chance we have for success. Understanding America's founding and the founding documents, especially the Constitution and The Bill of Rights, is a sure way to become an American forever. I know you love America as I do. Your author continually monitors what is happening to our government and he has written extensively on the major problems our country faces. Brian Kelly is one of America's most outspoken and eloquent conservative spokesmen.

Brian is the author of America 4 Dummmies; The Bill of Rights 4 Dummmies; No Amnesty! No Way!; The Annual Guest Plan; Saving America; Taxation Without Representation; Jobs! Jobs! Jobs!; The Federalist Papers, and many other patriotic books. All books are available at amazon.com/author/brianwkelly.

Like many Americans, Brian is fed up with stifling socialist progressive Marxists in the top seats in Washington. They place the needs of their buddies in front of the needs of Americans. Like many Americans, Kelly is shocked at how brazen the former administration was in ignoring our Constitution and our Bill of Rights! This must be stopped.

Brian W. Kelly has read the founding documents, the underlying intelligence reports, and he has researched and written about such topics for years. Brian has written one hundred nineteen other books and hundreds of patriotic articles. He is deeply concerned about how intolerable the results of poor government policy have been within our neighborhoods and our lives. His comprehensible and sane recommendations as brought forth in the Constitution and the Founding documents will contribute to this soon-to-be classic edition.

The Constitution by Hamilton, Jefferson, Madison, et al. is a title to get your attention for sure. I hope we got your attention. In addition to a review of the founding history, your author has presented the Constitution itself in a way that it can be easily read. The Constitution itself is a major civics lesson in this book and its intent is to bring you up to date on how to deal with the current national scene.

Additionally, Kelly has included copies of the founding documents so that you can read them directly in this book, rather than on the Internet.

You are going to love this book since it is designed by an American for Americans. Few books are a must-read but The Constitution by Hamilton, Jefferson, Madison, et al. will quickly appear at the top of America's most read list.

Sincerely,

Brian P. Kelly, Editor

Ch 1 What is the Constitution of the United States of America

Studying the Constitution

Welcome aboard this most patriotic book titled *The Constitution by Hamilton, Jefferson, and Madison, et al.* The words of these great patriots and others involved in the founding of our country as expressed in the Constitution form the basis for the government of the United States of America. It is the most fundamental document that describes America. It is also the supreme law of the land.

After several introductory chapters, we take you on a ride into the actual final draft of the US Constitution. As we reveal the Constitution as written, we also provide a number of helpful annotations to put in sharper focus the words of the founders who wrote this historical document.

If you desire some additional information before you begin this fantastic voyage, your author recommends another book that puts the Constitution into a historical perspective by describing the events of the day and the circumstances under which the Constitution was written. This book is titled *The Constitution Companion.* Its subtitle is *A Guide to Reading and Comprehending The Constitution of the United States of America*

Chapter 7 It's Time for the John Doe Party!

Brian W. Kelly

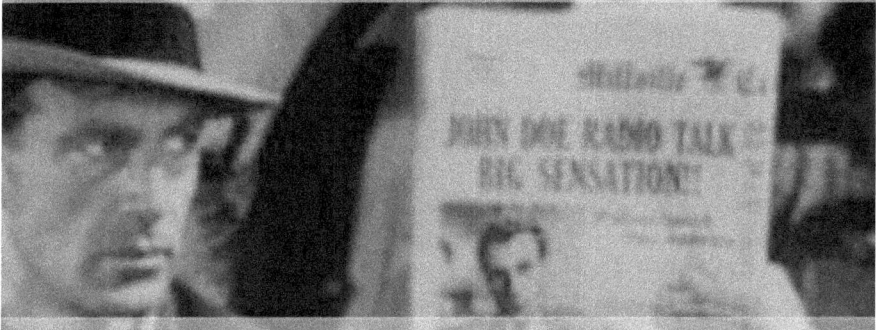

It's Time for The John Doe Party!

We can no longer count on Republicans for heavy lifting.

We can no longer count on Republicans for heavy lifting.

On Mayday, 2017, the Republican Party showed that the will of regular people in the Party matters not an iota. Republican elite leadership once again turned over the control of the budget to the Democrats. Hard as it is to believe, the truth is more difficult to assimilate than the fake news.

Ant-leftists, conservatives, nationalists, populists and regular Americans for America, who might very well be described simply as Trump voters and loyalists, learned a bitter lesson again watching Republican Party leaders give it up for the opposition party. We need a representative party that we can count on. That representation has not been delivered by the weak-kneed, elitist establishment Republican leadership. In the first budget submission of the Trump Administration, they found our backs and stabbed us again.

This book describes the values that are no longer important to Republicans and it offers a John Doe American solution so that the one-time Party of Lincoln is no longer important to everyday John Does. This book delivers a comprehensive rationale for why the Republican Party must be abandoned in favor of a brand new American Party that we would do well with the name The John Doe Party. The John Doe Party will soon be the rallying party for all the nobodies in America who love America. Gary Cooper and Frank Capra would call us all "John Does." The John Doe Party needs to replace the Republican Party. We do not need a Party that cannot be trusted?

Americans believed we threw out the swamp with Donald Trump's election yet, the elite establishment Republicans did not get the message. For example, anybody working on an Omnibus solution regarding the 2017 budget would have designed it to help build a better America. Republicans unfortunately are way too happy with Obamacare light, the baby killing Planned Parenthood, living without a secure Southern Wall, and the many other dictates imposed from donors and Republican Party elites who cannot understand the people's trust in President Trump.

The John Doe Party is the best choice for regular Americans.

Table of Contents

Preface:

Republicans were AWOL during the Obama presidency, and we quickly learned when they submitted their Mayday Budget in 2017 that the Party plan is to remain AWOL.

Once thought to be honest to a fault, the Republicans have taken to lying as a tool to survive. However, as neophytes in the lying game, they are not as good as Democrats, and they do not have the corrupt press available to back up everything they say.

Republicans chose a while ago to no longer care about the needs of any in the Republican Party other than the fat-cat donors and the K-street lobbyists, and the Party elites. They blamed conservatives for losing the Presidency in 2012, yet it was the Republican Party who backed an elite Republican not the anti-leftist conservatives, nationalists, populists, or regular Americans.

Though Mitt Romney was not a bad guy in 2012, and he may have made an OK president, he was not a good candidate for regular Americans, and he did not attract the masses of John Does to the Republican Party.

It really does not matter at this point as it is almost a certainty that Republicans for some time now have been looking for a new constituent base. Anti-leftist, non-elites without huge checkbook balances to the Republican Party today are passé. Wildly dreaming Republicans were hoping that Hispanics would become their new base, and Paul Ryan was commissioned to roll regular John Does off a cliff along with Granny.

While Republicans planned the demise of the little guys in the party, Americans who love America decided to launch a preemptive strike on the elite Republican establishment. We looked for and found a candidate that the wimpy, RINO, establishment Republicans did not want. That man of course is Donald Trump. He is now our President. His election shows that the people can do anything when motivated.

This book asks regular Americans such as anti-leftists, conservatives, nationalists, populists, independents, and regular American John Does who love America to strongly consider pulling out of the Republican Party. They have left us behind and they are not looking back to see if we are following. Even regular John Doe Democrats will be welcomed in The John Doe Party.

The good ole boy elite establishment Republicans can learn to swim in their own complacency. America-lovers, conservatives and former Tea Party people, who most often are one and the same, for eight years had a real enemy in the White House. His name as we well know is Barack Hussein Obama, and he had appointed his heir to be Hillary Rodham Clinton. Of course, we the people did not want that, and we made Donald Trump President of all America.

Why is this book about Republican leadership instead of the Democratic leadership? Democrats are always the clear and present danger to democracy. The answer hit me like a ton of bricks. It was a wake-up call. What seemed like out of nowhere, the GOP began to stop engaging Democrats as an opposition party by choosing not to help regular Americans fight the many Obama anti-American policies. Worse than that, with Trump's ascendancy to the presidency, the Republican RINOs continued to favor Democrats over the anti-leftists John Does that had always supported the Party of Lincoln.

It seemed like a bad dream when Republicans began to either believe they were dealt a winning hand in the Obama game or they were actually afraid of the President. Either way, these were scary times for Americans. No reinforcements came to the aid of Americans from the Republican Party, who had simply capitulated. Regular Americans now must get accustomed to getting nothing from Republicans. We must be prepared to go it alone. When Donald Trump showed up, we knew we had our leader; now we must fight to gain real representation.

For years, Americans believed that the Republican Party's values and our values were the same. Regular Americans have not had our own Party, and so for many years or so it seemed, Republicans were the enforcers for our values. Therefore, we logically believed that Republicans felt the same about important matters as we do. We were wrong. Republicans idiotically made their love affairs with the donor class and the K-street lobbyists well known and began to oppose regular Americans in important life and values matters.

In the Economy and in foreign affairs, Obama spent eight years in an anti-American role. During this time. The Republican leadership has been marking time choosing not to oppose the Democrats. Republicans became the great pretenders bluffing us that "our day would come," without any pushback to the Obama agenda.

That's why this book and The John Doe Party are so necessary today. We unabashedly recommend that Americans stop trusting Republican hand-shakers. They have proven that they will not fight for America or for American values. Their own greed trumps the needs of America. The leaders of the Grand Old Party have not even acknowledged that Obama and the Democrats are wrong. Anti-leftist regular Americans such as you and I must learn to go it along.

The sooner Americans can cast off Republicans as our only protection against Democrats and progressivism, the sooner we can move on to solving the problem for our values, our country, and our freedom. We need our own Party for sure; for without a Party, Regular John Doe Americans will not even be permitted to help on the battlefield when America is hanging by just a thread.

While we have been waiting for the right time to form a party, most of us think that we can defeat the Democrat leadership, the corporations, the unions, the media, and the traitorous Republicans who are not worth the ground they stand on. The time for waiting is over. It is now time to act.

As a great start, Americans from all political backgrounds chose to support Trump as our President. What a great move. He will govern as a good Republican, unless he too gets frustrated with the anti-Trump power brokers in the GOP and must rally the troops such as us, without the Republican Party umbrella. We must stand ready to do our part within a new Party—The John Doe Party.

We must work together to form The John Doe Party of John Doe Americans—the little guys in America, and leave the elite establishment to run its own party. Meanwhile, The John Doe Party takes all the regulars in America, including the regular Joe Democrats, Independents and members of other parties who love America. We can do it. Our first step was to get Trump elected and we did that. We the people can do anything. Now that we are motivated, it is time to move forward.

Brian W. Kelly for years and years has monitored what is happening to regular Americans and has written extensively on this major problem with the Republican Party. He is one of America's most outspoken and eloquent conservative on American values. He is the author of 116 books including Saving America The Trump Way, Why Trump? Taxation without Representation, Obama's Seven Deadly Sins, Kill the EPA! Jobs! Jobs! Jobs! and many other fine patriotic books.

All Kelly books are now available at Amazon, and Kindle. Many can be found at Barnes & Noble and other fine booksellers. www.amazon.com/author/brianwkelly. Like most of you, Brian is fed up with a stifling progressive liberal agenda in Washington that places the needs of everybody else in front of the needs of Americans who love America. Like many regular John Does, he is shocked at the behavior of the new RINO Republican Party.

Like you, Kelly is frustrated at how Republicans continually try to deceive us so that we will believe they are still with US on values and policy. They want our votes, but they no longer want to know what we think. It does not matter to these establishment elites.

Brian Kelly has read the intelligence reports, has researched and has written about these important topics for years, and he knows how intolerable the results of poor government policy can be within our neighborhoods. His comprehensible and sane recommendations in this book are explained in detail within the covers of this soon-to-be classic offering.

More and more Americans are clamoring for jobs but all that has been given by the prior President and his coterie was lip service. Republicans permitted it and are ready to fight President Donald Trump to assure there is no improvement. We cannot let this stand. Americans wanted to keep their health insurance and pick their own doctors. Yet, Republicans, who can help change this for

Americans have decided to cave to Democrats. Why was there no repeal of Obamacare?

Obama was a fine politician and he continues to make his case for his legacy. We cannot afford to be fooled again even if Republican leaders choose to continue sucking up to the Obama Shadow Government. Unbelievable as it may seem, Republicans have decided to give him what he wants by giving his legacy all the money they need to continue his agenda. The John Doe Party, when elected ASAP will end this practice.

It's Time for the John Doe Party! Is the bible to get us back on track with America. It shows why sucking up to RINO Republicans is bad for Americans, and Kelly tells us all what to do about it. You are going to love this book since it is designed by an American for Americans. Few books are a must-read but *It's Time for the John Doe Party!* has the prospects of ending the party of elites paid for by the US taxpayers.

Thanks to you, *It's Time for the John Doe Party!* is about to appear at the top of America's most read list.
Sincerely,

Brian P. Kelly, Editor

Regular Americans are mad as hell

Anti-left John Doe style regular Americans who once considered themselves pure bread conservatives are not alone in being upset today with many things, including a corrupt Congress, and an inept government. People of many political persuasions came out of the woodwork in late 2016 to express their outrage by voting for Donald Trump for President.

For eight years, the prior President, BHO, unlawfully bypassed the Constitution to do whatever he wanted to the country. Meanwhile wimpy Republicans in positions of power did not eve complain and actually appeared to be going along to get along. That made the John Does such as yours truly "Mad as Hell!"

Howard Beale in the paragraphs below represents all frustrated Americans. His story, though unrelated, really captures the mood and the emotions of America today regarding a government and a Republican Party gone bad!

You may not remember because you are probably not old enough but many others of you have enough years to have seen the movie long after its debut in 1976. So, if you have some baggage, and you have some time on your bones, you may remember back in November 1976 when Howard Beale, as played by Peter Finch, the long-time anchor in the movie "Network News," gets the bad news that eventually causes him to utter one of the most famous movie lines of all time.

Beale gets fired and is given two weeks. The long-time anchor has a very poor reaction to this news and he cannot control himself during the next news broadcast.

He promises to commit suicide on the air. The company immediately fires him—no second chances for a repeat performance. Beale is devastated and remorseful. He begs for the opportunity to say good-by to his fans with dignity, and he is reluctantly given his last opportunity ever for air time so that he can say his good-by's and also apologize. He gets his chance

Yet, once on the air, Beale is overwhelmed by his continuing circumstance. He goes into another diatribe starting off with a rant claiming that "Life is bullshit." He is so passionate that his ratings spike as he persuades his viewers to shout out of their windows: "I'm as mad as hell, and I'm not going to take this anymore!" That is the line heard 'round the world.

Well, my fellow Americans, I bet you saw this coming, and I am going to deliver it as passionately in words as I can: "I am mad as hell, and I am not going to take this anymore." I bet you are too. Let me remind you.

Taxes are too high; elected officials are out of touch; government is too big; spending is out of control; the Affordable Healthcare has become a train wreck; heroes are dying in the VA system, and nobody, after spending $160 billion per year supposedly on Veterans, can tell us why they are being neglected.

The people of America see the federal government for the last eight years as incompetent. We elected Republicans to have a voice, and yet we have no voice as they do what helps them and their elite donors, not us. Americans have no voice. We exchanged five top Taliban Officers from Gitmo for one deserter PFC. Additionally, and this is the worst: too many of US are too lazy to hold government accountable, and too many of our finest are on the take from elite donors and from insiders on K-Street.

It really is a train wreck. Corporate leaches have infiltrated our government and they seem to have a grip on Republican lawmakers. We have record unemployment; illegal aliens are smiling as they take American jobs; an unsustainable status quo supports special interests over the people's interests and when we look to the future we see a public education system that creates dummies and it trains k to 12 and college students to love the government. The graduates are so dumb that they don't seem to mind being called dummies. Scrooge would sum it up with a hearty "Bah Humbug." It is that bad!

We have had the poorest economy since the depression; excessive welfare; income and healthcare redistribution; institutionalized lying; a corrupt state-loving press carrying water for government; a debt large enough to kill America; huge student debt stopping graduates' successes; tyranny v. democracy; government lawlessness; support for criminals over police; freedom and liberty in jeopardy; American stagnation, and a big loss of America's world prestige.

And, on top of that, the press beats its breast about its importance by suggesting that the former president learned about what was happening across the world from reading the newspapers. Meanwhile government is spying on the people—even the newly elected president. Everybody in Washington gets a free ride with no accountability. It is that bad.

Our big government has become such a problem that most Americans believe that it can never again be the solution. Republicans choose to behave like Democrats rather than take them on. Our finest hope, our youth; go through colleges in huge numbers only to be unemployed and sacked with debt for life. As a Democrat, I am smarter than most. I know that the Democratic Party is the source of most ill fortune in the country. But, millennials do not believe it, so they are not willing to fight the bad guys in either party to make America great again!

This group of youngins known as millennials are the smartest by cranium but they are the stupidest offspring America has ever produced from anybody's loins in terms of their gullibility and their willingness to sacrifice their future for a promising promise.

They have no clue what life is about, and they actually protest American heroes such as Condoleezza Rice and Dr. Ben Carson. Both came to visit universities and were disrespected by the students. Rutgers for example in 2013 picked a boardwalk babe, Snooki, rather than an American who loves America to give them their final addresses at their Universities. Even Berkley will not permit free speech anymore and will not protect those who insist on it. The have small free speech zones on many college campuses so that free speech does not get in the way of their preferred propaganda. Hope is reserved for people who have never met today's millennials.

Students are guided by coffee-breath communist professors in universities and the students now accept that communism is OK. These are the elite progressives in their universities who believe free speech cannot be tolerated and who fill the heads of the millennials with mush. Their importance is endorsed by the universities when they get to be adorned in their finest plumage at commencement ceremonies, and they process before all others to the stage. With such guidance, students have learned that they really do know it all, though their parents have no clue what happens to them once they reach progressive campuses.

The student loan burden prevents former student borrowers from buying homes, cars, and having a family. Yet students do not blame their elite faculty and their establishment universities for anything. They blame George Bush for everything still because some talk show host once told them that works for him. They have begun to blame President Trump but gave Obama a free pass. It is great to have brains today, it is just not respected if one decides to use them for the public good.

Only retirees in their 90's can afford honeymoon cottages while looking for their next spouse. As many as 37 million student loan borrowers are too broke to engage in basic life. College loans, instead of lifting people to the top, have created a new race to the bottom,

On the International stage, America is a bad actor, and frustrated zealots from the left are making sure nobody gives America a break on the world stage. For eight years, the US tried to make the rest of the world strong by making America weak. The weaknesses of America are highlighted by a corrupt press because Americans have been doing too well and their perspective because of a new phenomenon known as "white privilege."

None of this helps command respect for our country from anybody but the guilt-ridden university students and their "lucky to have a job" mentors on the faculty. Having been a faculty member, I know how bad things are. The only people who seem to care have names like John Q. Public, John Doe, and Jane Doe. Thank you to the Johns and the Janes for choosing this book about a solution to the country's mess.

Nobody in the world gives America standing ovations anymore. Nobody asks us for curtain calls. Our leaders for eight years turned their backs on our friends and paid homage to our enemies. How is this? We now have a President who was elected to drain the swamp, but the Republican Congress seem to like living in the Swamp and they resist the President's overtures to make America great again.

Has Congress lost all its power? Or has Congress decided to simply give up. Who has the power in the US? The Constitution says it is the people! We replaced the President in 2016 and we must do the same for the Congress in 2018. If the Congress won't help the President drain the swamp, Congress should be taken out of their self-created swamp and sent back to live in an ungated community.

Before Donald Trump bombed the Syrian Airport and let the MOAB fly down on the caves, smaller and weaker countries such as Russia, Iran, and North Korea continued to push the US around and laugh at US, and our only response was to see if somehow it might have been because we may have offended them.

We once could not figure out any other way to show our greatness than by counting the number of hits on a *hashtag of **bring our girls home,*** when no Americans were missing, and we expected terrorists to cower when the number of twitter resends hits a million.

Over the last eight years, US officials refused to have an honest discussion about why four Americans, including the US Ambassador, were permitted to die in Benghazi when the military says they were prepared to save them. The then Secretary of State responsible for their deaths is then able to run for President as if their deaths did not matter. How does that happen in America? What Republican that you know spoke up about it?

We had an administration that blames the Christian Government of Nigeria for not reaching out enough to the Muslim killers who kidnapped 300 girls for sex slaves. Boko Haram had captured and killed 49 boys just a few weeks before.

The captors boldly announced they would sell them on the sex slave market, and the US was powerless in its feeble response. The new strategy is to have time go by so those who are at fault can claim that it is old news.

What has happened to our good sense? Should there not be a set of laws written by sane people so that insane acts cannot occur without retribution? Why do our representatives, especially Republicans who have lost heart not represent America?

For me, these are the worst days of America that I have ever witnessed. Yet, our recent government seemed to have no problems that need solutions. Clear-thinking Americans look at today's Republican leaders as buffoons, without the wherewithal to tie their own shoes. We yearned for a guy like Donald Trump to come forth to save us. And yet while he is prepared to do so, Republican Never Trumpers are willing to give America the five-finger salute to express their displeasure with our very capable President. These leaders would like all Americans to be happy in a state of mediocrity, rather than being outstanding. "Don't worry: Be Happy!"

If you have been paying attention, and I sure hope you have been as it is a civic duty, you know that there are even more issues than the exhaustive list we just walked you through. Isn't that a shame on US? I think this is the reason that you bought this book. Thank you very much. The Constitution is a survivor's guide to dealing with a corrupt nation; a corrupt press; a corrupt government and corrupt politicians who believe they can trick you into finding them acceptable. Armed with the Constitution, we John Does must get rid of the Republican party and replace it with a new party for us—for the people. Yes, the John Doe Party is the people's solution to corrupt greedy Republican elite politicians and their donor class.

Since you bought this book, I know you and I are on the right side and thankfully we are on the same side. Together, we can all help arrest control of our government back from perpetrators wishing to destroy US and a Republican Party that is determined not to lift a finger until we are destroyed from within.

We first must understand what is going on and we then must understand our rights. Even before you and me and everybody else are on board, just like Howard Beale, we must start the first wave of solutions by opening our windows all the way and shouting as loud as we all can: "I am mad as hell, and I am not going to take this anymore."

Then, we must make sure that we talk to everybody we know on the streets, supermarkets, and the neighborhoods—people like you and I and others, and let's help them all know that unless we all fully engage in America, when we wake up from our deep fog, there may be no America left for our progeny. We will have blown it for sure if that is permitted to happen.

Getting The John Doe Party off the ground is a great start.

Ch 2 Heritage Foundation Says Don't Be Snookered.

Republicans still snooker the people

Republicans were once solid on doing what was right for America. Democrats always talked the better game but handed the outhouse spoon to Americans as the fulfillment of their promise. After Americans voted in Donald Trump and a Republican House and Senate with the expressed purpose of draining the swamp, Republicans chose not to make it happen. In its first noteworthy act of this Congressional session, the Republican leadership decided to protect the swamp and drain the people of any financial influence in the government. No, I am not kidding.

The Heritage Foundation supports regular Americans. They put together an analysis of the Republican charade. They wrote a great synopsis of the message sent by Republican Elites on Mayday, 2017 in the Omnibus Budget. The Republicans supported every Democrat notion that Obama had put in his budget from last year, and even some Obama had forgotten. And, they gave the Democrats 1.1 Billion spending money for whatever they wanted. But, they provided the people with no wall and they refused to begin draining the swamp. Doesn't that upset you? Doesn't that make you mad as hell. The Republicans betrayed the people.

Here is a piece written by Heritage. You will be further enraged after you digest what the Republicans just did to us

KEY VOTE: "NO" ON FY17 OMNIBUS SPENDING BILL (H.R. 244)

MAY 02, 2017

This week, the House and Senate will consider the Consolidated Appropriations Act of 2017 (H.R. 244), a 1,665-page omnibus spending package that would fund the federal government through September 30, 2017. The Heritage Foundation explains that while the bill, which was released publicly at 2 AM Monday morning, "does make progress" on some issues, "it woefully fails the test of fiscal responsibility and does not advance important conservative policies."

Many conservatives went along with a short-term continuing resolution last December based on a promise that the current deadline would be used to advance key policy priorities. Instead, the bill is widely viewed as a rebuke to President Trump's agenda and conservative priorities.

Overall, the Trump administration requested an additional $30 billion in military, $1.5 billion to continue construction of the southern border wall, and $18 billion in discretionary cuts. The bill provides only $15 billion for defense (of which $2.5 billion is withheld until the administration submits a plan to combat ISIS), provides no funding for the border wall, and actually increases domestic discretionary spending. Through a combination of emergency funding and overseas contingency operations funds, the bill pushes discretionary spending $93 billion above the budget caps.

The Trump administration was rebuked at the program level as well. The Department of Energy's Office of Science will receive an additional $42 million, whereas the administration requested a $900 million reduction. Funding for Community Development Block Grants was kept level despite a $1.5 billion requested reduction. The list goes on, as CQ Roll Call reported: "Trump proposed killing off more than a dozen federal programs in his fiscal 2018 budget outline, but it doesn't appear appropriators are inclined to reduce or eliminate federal funding for any of those line items."

Liberals celebrated the bill as a victory over President Trump and claimed they successfully blocked "more than 160 Republican poison pill riders." Heritage notes the omnibus "fails to advance almost any key conservative policies" as "it would continue to provide funding for Planned Parenthood and do nothing to restrict funding to sanctuary cities."

Along with a lack of conservative policy riders, the bill contains a $1.3 billion bailout for the United Workers of America, a union that represents about 10 percent of all coal production in the U.S. today. Coal miners deserve proper health care and retirement benefits, but it is the job of the union and private companies that made those promises, not taxpayers, to provide those benefits.

H.R. 244 contains a second health care bailout to Puerto Rico. In passing a bill to help Puerto Rico restructure its debts last year, lawmakers promised there would be no cash bailout. Yet, this bill would give the mismanaged and politically corrupt Puerto Rican government $296 million in taxpayer dollars to cover their shortage in Medicaid funds.

Coupled with these two bailouts, the omnibus spending bill also funds liberal priorities and initiatives. H.R. 244 includes millions in increased funding for Department of Energy (DOE) pet projects, national parks, Amtrak, Head Start, college tuition assistance, the National Endowments for the Arts and Humanities, the Transportation Security Administration (TSA), and even a Bureau of Land Management (BLM) sage grouse conservation project.

When spending bills provide more funding to the National Institutes of Health (NIH) than border security, as this bill does, it's fair for conservatives to ask if this resembles more of an Obama administration-era spending bill than a Trump one.

The Heritage Foundation's Justin Bogie and Rachel Greszler acknowledge the bill "does make progress" on some issues, but they add:

"Unfortunately, the additional $15 billion in defense spending is only half of what President Donald Trump requested earlier this year and is inadequate to meet global threats facing the country.

"The additional $1.5 billion for border security is important in the battle to curb illegal immigration. However, none of these funds can be used for construction of a border wall, one of the president's top priorities.

"Unfortunately, none of the increases in spending proposed by this bill would be offset. Earlier this year, the president released a 'skinny budget' which proposed $18 billion in 2017 cuts, yet none of those cuts made it into the latest budget deal."

Heritage Action opposes H.R. 244 and will include it as a key vote on our legislative scorecard.

Ch 3 Republicans Have Betrayed Their Voters!

Who do you trust?

As discussed in Chapter 2, The House was wrapping up negotiations on the big Omnibus the Sunday before Mayday 2017. It was a joint effort of the Congress (House) of the United States and the President, held behind closed doors. The result was that the Republicans agreed to stiff the American people on the extension of the 2017 budget known as the Omnibus.

Americans have become accustomed to lies and even bigger lies from our elected officials but few of us expected President Trump to join the party. We hope our President is working on a special deal but right now, to a lot of regular Americans, it seems that we have been the victims of a major prevarication that was not an accident.

The official word from whitehouse.gov is as follows: **"If the Consolidated Appropriations Act, 2017 were presented to the President in its current form, his advisors would recommend that he sign the bill into law."** We can only pray that our real President reappears, takes the Heritage Foundation's advice, and vetoes this bill. At the same time, let's hope the President of the US sends the President of the Swamp, Special Interests, and the Republican Leadership back into hiding.

We all know that there could be no budget celebration this week without President Trump going along with the partiers just to get along. It surely does not sound like the modus operandi of our formerly tough and triumphant head of state. Maybe it is just part of deal-making, but many anti-leftists are very concerned.

It is killing folks like me that our President is now taking cues from swamp people—most of whom are Republican Party wimps and long-term Trump haters. What is up?

One school of thought says that the President has resigned himself into believing that he can eat crow dinners in perpetuity and his loyal constituents such as you and me, will not notice. They are dead wrong. Mr. President, we have noticed. We can see the feathers between your teeth. I am sorry to say.

None of us are happy about the new you. Bring back the old Donald J. Trump, please even though the new you is much better than Obama. Yes, we blame the Republican House Leadership first, but they can't have their way without your full complicity.

What happened Mr. President to your toughness and excess mettle. Please go back into the drawer where you put your good stuff, and take it out again and start wearing it again. We still need you and we will forgive you. You are not one of them. Please do not become one of them for too long.

Democrats, of course, have claimed a huge victory that they blocked the Trump agenda. That is not good news. They are our opponents.

For the first time in years, this time, they are telling the truth. They did block the Trump agenda and substituted their own. It was a masterful trick for a bunch of losers. Their clear budget victory took the wind out of the sails of a lot of hopeful Trump loyalists.

Americans expect nothing from Democrats and so there is little anger against them. Republicans offered real American regular people hope, but they chose to fail again on purpose as they really do not want the swamp to be drained. It's tough to believe Republicans will ever get the people's wish list done. You remember that list—it was once Donald Trump's to-do-list.

The day before Mayday, campaign promises no longer mattered. This gave the Democrats their victory and that was all that mattered to lying Republicans who for years asked for one more thing and one more thing to have enough power to fight the Democrats. Now, with more than enough power, they decided to implement the Democratic agenda saying to hell with the people "what brung us."

To be sure the news was true, many Americans went back to the stories of the election day results and they learned again that the Democrats did not win. So, if they did not win, why are they able to keep beating up Republicans? Answer: Only because the Republicans want to be beaten up!

The Republicans did it all without the help of Democrats, but it pleases the Democrats to no end. The Republican Party showed that the vote of the people did not matter an iota as they willingly and gleefully turned over the control of the precious US budget to the same Democrats, who had lost it all in the last election. Yes, the Democrats who blamed the Russians for their loss. Same Democrats. The people had voted but their representatives did not choose to hear the message. Hard as it is to believe, the truth is more difficult sometimes to assimilate than the fake news.

Anti-left Americans as well as nationalists, populists, and of course Americans for America, who might very well be described simply as Trump voters, swamp-drainers, and Trump loyalists learned a bitter lesson again in trusting Republicans to do the right thing. When the news eked out that the Democrats had a big budget win, it was also known that the people had a big loss because the Republicans chose to have a big budget loss. Republicans had the power and they voted to lose.

This is a story told often in the last six years of Obama times. Republicans offered one excuse after another as Obama and company were ripping apart America. Republicans tried to explain it away by saying it was necessary to get any deal. A bad deal is not a deal, it is a giveaway.

Rather than forcing the Democrats to shut down our poorly run government, cowardly Republicans chose to give them it all. Republican double dealers even gave Democrats little things that the President really wanted just to rub salt in his wounds. The Congressional leadership does not act like they like our President. Maybe we need to replace them.

The Omnibus Bill seemed to be written by the staffs of the Donor class, Lobbyists and K-street insiders to keep their coffers full and say: "to the nether world with the American people." Then the shrewd Republican Never-Trump leadership claimed a victory after giving the house away. They continue to hope the people are stupid and that we believe they really won and the Democrats lost. Not even close. The Dems scored a big one. The Republicans took a fall for their donors who like the swamp.

When you read about the bill, for you won't want to read the 1600+ pages of government-ese, in which you will specifically see how the President and the people were stiffed. For example, as noted in the brief Heritage analysis, the bill provides only $15 billion for defense (of which $2.5 billion is withheld until the administration submits a plan to combat ISIS).

The bill provides no funding for the border wall. Yes, that's right, Trump's #1 issue! He was stiffed on that too. The bill actually increases domestic discretionary spending. Through a combination of emergency funding and overseas contingency operations funds, the bill pushes discretionary spending $93 billion above the budget caps. Democrats love the spending increases. The people did not win on this one.

The Trump administration was rebuked at the program level as well. The Never-Trumpers gave The Department of Energy's Office of Science an additional $42 million. That seems like nothing until you learn that Trump had requested a $900 million reduction. Funding for Community Development Block Grants was kept level despite a $1.5 billion requested reduction. The list goes on. For example, CQ Roll Call reported in early May that:

"Trump proposed killing off more than a dozen federal programs in his fiscal 2018 budget outline, but it doesn't appear appropriators are inclined to reduce or eliminate federal funding for any of those line items." Whatever Lola wanted, Lola did not get. Neither did President Trump. Why the President seems happy about this claptrap is the enigma of our times.

Swamp drainers from around the country asked themselves whether the budget results would have been much different if they had voted for Hillary instead of Donald Trump.

The Swamp drainers, for want of a better nickname--Democrat and Republican alike, would cry loud about this face if they believed that anybody would listen. They would scream that the Trumpists need a Party that is there for the regular people in America, not the big shot Trump haters.

Somehow, despite a people's victory in November, it is clear that the Democrats, the Trump-haters in the Republican-majority Congress, the K-Street lobbyists, the donor base, and even the US Chamber of Commerce were able to overpower the administration into accepting not much more than nothing in the 1.1 Trillion Omnibus budget.

The President seems to believe that this group will all be on his side in October and they will pass his 2018 budget or vote to shut down the government. Chances of seeing any Trump programs implemented ever went down by 99% after the Republican cave-in on the Omnibus bill.

The US Chamber of Commerce is not often singled out as being bad guys. Yet, they are scum. Sorry, that is how I see it. Michele Malkin, a noted anti-leftist, describes them quite succinctly:

"The U.S. Chamber of Commerce is a politically entrenched synod of special interests. These fat cats do not represent the best interests of American entrepreneurs, American workers, American parents and students, or Americans of any race, class, or age who believe in low taxes and limited government. The chamber's business is the big business of the Beltway, not the business of mainstream America."

I sure wish I had written that. Michele Malkin is one of the good ones.

Can you imagine the fierceness of the snakes in the swamp that are trying to take Donald Trump and the rest of us down with them? Don't ever trust the US Chamber of Commerce. They are anti-American, pro-greed, and as selfish as selfish can be defined.

The type of political party that the anti-leftist swamp-drainers need in order to win back America is definitely not the one controlled today by the weak-kneed, wimpish, elitist establishment Anti-Trump Republicans. They have had the power in the past but have consistently made excuses for not doing what the people voted for.

For years, they deferred to the whims of Barack Obama and his many budgets and his continued excessive spending. This time, they simply took the old Obama budget from 2016, dusted it off, blessed it and said it was good. They snuck this through as if there was not one good and honest Republican left in the Congress, who would stand up and support the needs of the people. Maybe they were right.

Those wanting Trump to stick to his guns would tell any reporter that Republicans have not done it for us. In their first chance to set a budget for the Trump Administration, the supposed Party of Lincoln found our backs and stabbed us again by choice. Lincoln, the first Republican President, and a great one in American History, would have done much better.

This is a betrayal of the people. The values of anti-leftists and like-minded Americans are no longer important to Republicans. Republicans simply cannot be trusted. We know this from history. So, what can we the people do? We can say good-by to the Republican Party. We can end the charade

We cannot afford to trust Republicans ever again. What we need is a solution for regular John Does—those of us out here in Realville, not Plasticville. We need a John Doe solution so that the Republican leadership no longer needs to be important to us, the regular every day citizens of America.

And, so there is a compelling rationale for why the Republican Party must be abandoned in favor of a brand new American Political Party. A great name for this new Party is "The John Doe Party," as we John Does are the people to be represented by this new Party. To repeat, Republicans simply cannot be trusted. In their hearts, Republicans must be wondering why we ever trusted them.

The John Doe Party can be designed to be the party for all the nobodies in America. Gary Cooper and Frank Capra would call these nobodies like you and I, "John Does." That is who we are, and the Republicans make sure that we know it every time they have a chance.

The John Doe Party needs to replace the Republican Party as a mainstream political party. Who needs a party that cannot be trusted? Democrats seem happy with the Democratic Party so this essay in this chapter is not directly about them, However, lots of Democrats are John Does like you and I for sure and though they do not trust Republicans, they would more than likely welcome a change to an open and honest group who have their best interests at heart. They are sick of dishonest government just as we anti-leftists.

The irony in losing this budget battle is that in November 2016, anti-communist and anti-leftist Americans believed that we had begun the elimination of the Washington swamp simply by electing Donald Trump. Yet, the elite establishment Republicans did not care to hear and absorb the people's clear message.

Anybody working on a solution regarding the US budget in its Omnibus form, would have brought it in long before May 1, and it would be for the people who won. It would not favor a group that had lost the election.

Slimy RINO Republican leaders unfortunately were way too happy with what the Democrats had done for the past eight years. Their budget showed an affinity for funding Obamacare, funding the baby killing Planned Parenthood, funding Sanctuary Cities, and bringing more "refugees" into America—and of course living without a secure Southern border with an impenetrable and beautiful wall—along with many other dictates from their Trump-hating donors and the special interests on K Street deep in the heart of the swamp.

Of course, the Republican Party for years has turned on its base whenever it was convenient. This is nothing new. Now, while they turn on the people who elected the President, they do so by joining Democrats in demeaning President Trump. They have decided to not permit the President or the people to gain the fruits of their election victory over the Democrats and the swamp establishment.

Too many Republicans in powerful positions hate President Trump more than they hate terrorists and more than they fear that one day they may be thrown out of office. The people therefore must show strength. We must act to shut-down Republican leaders by creating a new Party and then by denying these traitors the right to represent the people ever again.

The John Doe Party is the vehicle to get America right again. Republican leaders abhor the people's trust in Donald Trump, and have served themselves rather than their constituents. They will not be missed, even by the President. And, so the people, the John Does like you and I in the real world must join in to shut the Republican Elite out of any new party that we may form and any new government that we may elect.

Americans do not have to keep taking it on the chin. We have a real choice –**The John Doe Party.**

The immortal Gary Cooper would never let us down. Let's all try to see "Meet John Doe" soon. Viewing this classic movie will assure us that the Washington elites have not served the John Does or Jane Does of America for many, many years. We can change that. We can be the John Doe Club, the John Doe Movement, and the John Doe Party that wins America back for Americans.

When we meet John Doe in the great Capra movie, we will all better understand what being an American is all about! John Doe Democrats and John Doe Republicans, who have seen both political parties abandon the people, will have a choice once again.

It won't be easy, but Americans can do anything. It is time to dump the Party of Lincoln. Lincoln would be ashamed of them and demand nothing less to protect his name. Republicans no longer are worthy of our trust, and we, the John Does of America matter.

Let's quickly bring on the John Doe Party

Ch 4, not shown in this synopsis, introduces John Doe, as portrayed by Gary Cooper in the movie. What an inspiring thought! Enjoy as you turn the page.

Other books by Brian Kelly: (amazon.com, and Kindle)

Taxation Without Representation Can the US Afford Another Tea Party?
Delete the EPA You won't believe what they are up to now!
Wipe Out All Student Debt Now! How to improve the economy with one bold move
 Boost Social Security Now! Hey Buddy Can You Spare a Dime?
The Birth of American Football. From the first college game in 1869 to the last Super Bowl
Obamacare: A One-Line Repeal Congress must get this done.
A Wilkes-Barre Christmas Story A wonderful town makes Christmas all the better
A Boy, A Bike, A Train, and a Christmas Miracle a Christmas story that will melt your heart
Pay-to-Go America-First Immigration Fix
Legalizing Illegal Aliens Via Resident Visas Americans-first plan saves $Trillions. Learn how!
60 Million Illegal Aliens in America!!! A simple, America-first solution.
The Bill of Rights by Founder James Madison Refresh *your knowledge of the specific rights for all*
It's time for the John Doe Party! Republicans can no longer handle the load.
Great Players in Army Football Great Army Football played by great players..
Great Coaches in Army Football Army's coaches are all great.
Great Moments in Army Football Army Football at its best.
Great Moments in Florida Gators Football Gators Football from the start. This is the book.
Great Moments in Clemson Football CU Football at its best. This is the book.
Great Moments in Florida Gators Football **Gators** Football from the start. This is the book.
The **Constitution Companion.** A Guide to Reading and Comprehending the Constitution
The Constitution by Hamilton, Jefferson, & Madison – Big type and in English
PATERNO: The Dark Days After Win # 409. Sky began to fall within days of win # 409.
JoePa 409 Victories: Say No More! Winningest Division I-A football coach ever
American College Football: The Beginning From before day one football was played.
Great Coaches in Alabama Football Challenging the coaches of every other program!
Great Coaches in Penn State Football the Best Coaches in PSU's football program
Great Players in Penn State Football The best players in PSU's football program
Great Players in Notre Dame Football The best players in ND's football program
Great Coaches in Notre Dame Football The best coaches in any football program
Great Players in Alabama Football from Quarterbacks to offensive Linemen Greats!
Great Moments in Alabama Football AU Football from the start. This is the book.
Great Moments in Penn State Football PSU Football, start--games, coaches, players,
Great Moments in Notre Dame Football ND Football, start, games, coaches, players
Cross Country With the Parents A great trip from East Coast to West with the kids
Seniors, Social Security & the Minimum Wage. Things seniors need to know.
How to Write Your First Book and Publish It with CreateSpace
The US Immigration Fix--It's all in here. Finally, an answer.
I had a Dream IBM Could be #1 Again The title is self-explanatory
WineDiets.Com Presents The Wine Diet Learn how to lose weight while having fun.
Wilkes-Barre, PA; Return to Glory Wilkes-Barre City's return to glory
Geoffrey Parsons' Epoch... The Land of Fair Play Better than the original.
The Bill of Rights 4 Dummmies! This is the best book to learn about your rights.
Sol Bloom's Epoch ...Story of the Constitution The best book to learn the Constitution
America 4 Dummmies! All Americans should read to learn about this great country.
The Electoral College 4 Dummmies! How does it really work?
The All-Everything Machine Story about IBM's finest computer server.
ThankYou IBM! This book explains how IBM was beaten in the computer marketplace by neophytes

Brian has written 146 books in total. Other books can be found at amazon.com/author/brianwkelly

www.ingramcontent.com/pod-product-compliance
Lightning Source LLC
Chambersburg PA
CBHW070852280326
41934CB00008B/1410